THE BOOK OF
ARABIC WISDOM
Proverbs & Anecdotes

Compiled by Hussain Mohammed Al-Amily

Interlink Books

An imprint of Interlink Publishing Group, Inc.
Northampton, Massachusetts

First American edition published in 2005 by

INTERLINK BOOKS
An imprint of Interlink Publishing Group, Inc.
46 Crosby Street, Northampton, Massachusetts 01060
www.interlinkbooks.com

First published in the UK by New Internationalist Publications Ltd., 2003

Library of Congress Cataloging-in-Publication Data
The book of Arabic wisdom : proverbs & anecdotes / compiled by Hussain
Mohammed Al-Amily—1st American ed.
p. cm.
ISBN 1-56656-582-0 (pbk.)
1. Proverbs, Arabic—Translations into English. 2. Quotations,
Arabic—Translations into English. I. Amily, Hussain Mohammed, 1927–
PN6519.A7B66 2004
398'.9927—dc22
2004016953

Cover illustration by Rowena Dugdale
Printed and bound in Canada by Webcom

To request our complete 40-page full-color catalog,
please call us toll free at **1-800-238-LINK,** visit our
website at **www.interlinkbooks.com**, or write to
Interlink Publishing
46 Crosby Street, Northampton, MA 01060
e-mail: info@interlinkbooks.com

To our late illiterate mother who strove and suffered to teach us – her eight children – to 'read and write'.

AND to remember Abu Abid, the tiller – driven out of the Euphrates, he came to be cast down on the shores of the Tigris – whose wisdom, sad humor and ever-smiling courage inspired me to initiate this work.

A noble man cannot be indebted for his culture to a narrow circle; the world and his native land must act on him.
– GOETHE

CONTENTS

Squeeze the past like a sponge, smell the present like a rose and send a kiss to the future.

INTRODUCTION

Crossing a field along the Euphrates, the story goes, a prince passed an elderly peasant planting a young sapling in the soil. The prince was curious and stopped to ask the man why he cared to plant a tree whose fruit he was too old to reap. 'They planted and we ate; we plant and they will eat,' responded the old farmer. The prince admired the answer and rewarded him with a thousand gold pieces. 'You see, the tree has borne fruit already, Your Highness,' said the old planter. Once again the prince ordered a present for him and asked the entourage to proceed. 'See! The tree has borne twice even before it has matured.' The prince had to give a third reward and hurried away before his treasure was exhausted by the old man's wit.

Shared heritage

On a trip around the Asiri countryside, a hilly region of unspoiled natural beauty in Saudi Arabia, one recent sunny winter, we were comfortably seated on the divan near a fireplace at our elderly host Abu Abood's. Through small deep windows on the third floor of his guest house, we overlooked a clean white courtyard below, and a hilly green landscape rolling on to meet the horizon. We sipped pure Arabic coffee, yellowish and thick, with Bishar dates, telling stories of great floods that had filled the valleys of Asir, of past wanderings in the vast deserts stretching from behind the mountains that soared high around us, and of the cave-dwellers, Beni-Mwailik, who have had unwillingly to abandon their time-honored cliff dwellings for the nearby village the government has built for them. We gazed on the Poet's Mountain ahead of us and remembered the tale of the three pretty maidens who had craved to scale the peak to meet him and be praised in his passionate verses.

Although we were a mixed company of travelers there at Abu Abood's, the moment was special. We felt we were joyfully rediscovering ourselves as fellow Arabs with basic things in common. The artificial barriers that had kept us apart had fallen away. I for one had a warm feeling as if I were at home; that warmth was enhanced when we embellished our conversation with proverbs – a customary manner of talking amongst Arabs.

Sayings, known to me from my homeland of Iraq, thrive in almost identical forms in other Arab countries I have visited, despite the physical distance and political events that have set some of us apart in the past.

Live and see, move around and see more, as we are wont to say.

Or *Your luck may get sick, but it won't die.*

Ancient and modern

I have been fascinated by how standard Arabic, which is often formal and literary, can be enriched by more colloquial utterances of pure Arabic form. This drew me towards folk sayings which are a rich and inexhaustible source. Packed in concise, eloquent, witty or ironic modes of expression, and kept

place in present times what with the booming arms trade and plans for Star Wars); or *If you don't lower down your basket, no-one will fill it for you*. Nevertheless the wisdom they impart doesn't lack a universal resonance.

Arabic usage, although often embroidered by various flowery figures of speech, also has a laconic side, and it is this which comes to the fore in this selection of proverbs and amusing anecdotes.

As proverbs slowly emerge and evolve, many which are as ancient as Arabic culture itself are still in everyday use, although understandably they are often meant to be applied in figurative senses. Some may well have been defeated by time. These days you would be unlikely to hear someone intent on declaring war ironically lamenting that *The bows are in Persia and the arrows will come soon!* about their lack of preparation for the event.

About the translations

I have attempted to stay within the frontiers of my native modes of expression, thus preserving, I hope, much of the original flavor of the Arabic versions.

Most of the material appears here in original translations from Arabic sources. However several proverbs from the wider Islamic world are also included; there are proverbs of Sumerian (an ancient Iraqi civilization), Kurdish, Persian, Turkish, Afghan, Tunisian and Uzbek origins. There are also proverbs from Andalusia in Spain and Malta, both of which have historic connections to the Arab world. Specific regional Arabic origins have been indicated when they are of particular interest, like when they relate to customs or the weather. Some *hadith* or sayings of the Prophet Muhammad, founder of Islam, as traditionally recounted in Islamic

constantly embellished from generation to generation, proverbs reflect the entire range of human experience in short sentences. They may also guide us in tracing the kinship bonds of ethnic or cultural-social groups, as is the case amongst Arab peoples. Proverbs are stores of information and a showroom of truth, although they sometimes contradict one another: *Do no good lest you receive bad (in return)* which contrasts sharply with the injunction to *Do good and throw into the sea (one day it will return your way)*. Sometimes they are the tips of anecdotes and at others they reflect attitudes cultivated through no-nonsense dealings with life's realities: *Every goat is hanged by its trotters*; or *Scratch me, I scratch you!*

To the Western reader, some may evoke an exotic ancient world. For instance: *Ride a donkey to take you to the camel* (the modern equivalent for which would be taking a taxi to the airplane); or *Don't go to a fight, nor gather stones for fighters* (which seems a bit out of faith, are also included. There are quatrains by two eleventh-century poets – the Persian Omar Khayyam (as translated by Fitzgerald) and Abul Alaa Al-Ma'arri (in original translations), who is less known in the West but who is believed to have been close friends with Khayyam. Also some couplets by Sheikh Sadi of Shiraz, a famous thirteenth century Sufi mystic (mainly translated by Edward B Eastwich) and several of his prose maxims have also been quoted. One will also encounter Bahlool, a satiric figure from folklore, a kind of wise fool who revealed the underlying truth of various social situations in ancient Baghdad.

Where the intent of a proverb may not be immediately evident, I have provided comments in brackets to help the reader. I have also taken the liberty of including some of my own reflections, attributed to Lilminber which translates as 'by the platform speaker'. This I was for some years, when I spent time as a young mullah roving

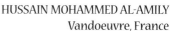

the countryside of my beloved homeland, Iraq, giving sermons to the beautiful peoples of the Tigris and Euphrates, from a chair or pulpit ('minber').

Proverbs are a universal manifestation of human wisdom, humor, customs and myths, common to all the peoples of the world. They have been my passion since I was a small boy living in a Lebanese village decades ago. Well-spoken villagers uttered them in their endless mirthful chatting, in the tales they liked to tell me. Then, years later, back in Iraq, I was enchanted by witty, laconic folk sayings that came as naturally as breathing air to some people, although spoken in the other flavor of the Iraqi dialect. In venturing to introduce a collection emanating from the vast variety of the Arab and Islamic world, I hope to open a window upon the soul of an old culture that is still lively and flourishing.

Translating proverbs is not the easiest of tasks, especially not from Arabic into a Western language. Hence, liberal translation was sometimes inevitable, and on the whole I had to seek assistance in checking my texts. This I thankfully received from my 'Samideanos' (Esperanto fellow-thinkers): Douglas Norman, James A Pasquill, W J Thorne, and from Dr John Wolfard, whose appreciation greatly encouraged me to persevere with this work. Thanks is also due here to the Management of the Centre Cultural André Malraux in Vandoeuvre (Les-Nancy), France, for their assistance by placing at my disposal some of the Centre's helpful facilities which considerably eased my work.

HUSSAIN MOHAMMED AL-AMILY
Vandoeuvre, France

Editor's note

In their English form, and perhaps as a result of translation, many of the proverbs in this selection were male in perspective and values. In many cases, this is how they evolved, reflecting roles and power relationships in the Arabic world. The use of terms such as 'he' or 'man' may have been taken to include women by those who originated, collected or translated the proverbs. However, today such language is offensive to many people, men and women alike. Bearing this in mind, many of the proverbs in this collection have been 'translated' once more to reflect a wider humanity. Nevertheless, some proverbs that quite clearly delineate gender expectations in the culture from which they arise are also included as a gesture towards greater comprehensiveness.

The quotations included, mainly from ancient authors, reflect the eclectic choice of the compiler Hussain Mohammed Al-Amily (who uses the *nom-de-plume* Lilminber for his own contributions in the book) and supplement the traditional wisdom of the proverbs. A survey of Arabic quotations was not the intention. There are numerous Qur'anic quotations and *hadith*, which are the traditions of the Prophet Muhammad, serving as a guide for Islamic peoples around the world. Also included are numerous anecdotes of Bahlool, a wise fool from Iraqi folklore.

A

Amongst all the able, none are so powerless as those who will not act
— AL-MUTANABI, tenth century poet

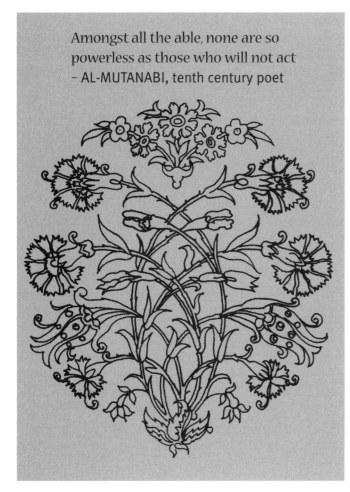

Ability has no school. –
TURKISH

Some are unable to do a thing, but some things are impossible to do.
– IBN RUSHD, tenth century Andalusian philosopher

Power without education is deplorable, and education without power is in vain.
– SHEIKH SADI, thirteenth century Persian Sufi poet

Tell her she can do it, and she can.

Ability has limits, possibility has none.
– Lilminber

ABSENCE

Absence is a cause of estrangement.

A man went away and came back with fortunes, a woman was absent and came back with tears.

If estrangement doesn't break you, it will strengthen you.
– TUNISIAN

Neither Abu Ali nor his spade (were there)!
– IRAQI
[Of someone who, though long-awaited, remains absent.]

The absent one carries his excuse with him.

Present in body, absent in mind.

ABILITY

If a camel staggers under a heavy load, put it on two donkeys.

A thousand dogs can't catch up with a gazelle.

Send your son to the market place and see what he can do.

Although God is Almighty, He never sends rain down from a clear sky. – AFGHAN

1

A

If a bird went away, its nest would be removed.

The absent one's angels are still present.
[One should not backbite or misjudge an absent person.]

Forgetfulness is absence, remembrance is presence.

Going away is your decision; coming back won't be.

The sparrow whose (tethering) thread is cut...
[Of someone who will never return.]

ACQUAINTANCE

People are planks until they are acquainted with one another.

The face you meet every day you must not displease in any way.

You saw my face, you saw my backside.
[You know me well now.]

First befriend the dog. – MALTESE

ACTION

A little hole can sink a big ship.

If you are an anvil sustain; if you are a hammer strike.

One stone can disturb a flock of birds.

A pebble can support a big jar, but a big jar can't bear a pebble (when thrown at it).

If someone can cook a meal by their sweet talk, then I can make butter flow like a river.
– PERSIAN

A pair of bees can do more than a bag of flies.
– TURKISH

Unless opposed to the Devil, secret actions are devilish. – PERSIAN

Press the clay whilst it is soft and plant the sapling whilst it is green.
[The Arabic equivalent of 'Strike while the iron is hot'.]

Eat me like a lion, but don't bite me like a dog.

The sword is longest when wielded.

If your sword is broken, make a sickle out of it.

One foot within, another foot without.
[Of hesitation.]

Tell them to act, and God will see their actions.
– THE QUR'AN

ACTIVITY

In movement there is gain.

A

A walker is a bird; the indolent one is but a stone.

Activity is the spring of life. – PERSIAN

ADVENTURE

If you put your house on fire, you will warm up with it once.

He who likes to eat honey must suffer the stings of bees; he who covets a married woman must be prepared for trouble.

Wretched is the adventurous one, even if he stays safe.

She who stands at the edge is about to fall.

ADVERSITY

God sends adversities and consolations together.
[OR: God sends us tests and He helps us pass them.]

There is no tree that has not been shaken by a storm.

After black there is no (darker) color. – SHEIKH SADI, thirteenth century Persian Sufi poet
[After a mishap, one can only hope for relief.]

Here is a woe that makes you weep and there is another that makes you laugh.

One woe is better than two.

To see heaven, the ant must fall on its backside.

Adversities are the touchstone of humanity.

The ceiling always falls on the poor person's head.

The wind of adversity doesn't suffocate the house of wisdom.

When the chariot is broken, many will come to show you the route.

AFFLUENCE

If a wall didn't fall, a well wouldn't be filled up.

Until you've walked across the sands, don't sleep on a bed of silk sheets. – PERSIAN

Too much of a thing is like too little of it.

The sea doesn't buy fish.

Abundance is the perverter of reason.
– SHEIKH SADI, thirteenth century Persian Sufi poet

Earn your living and keep well
and let the greedy go to Hell.

AGE

If you want to know his age, open his mouth.
[Apparently of a donkey, but by implication also of people, ie let them talk.]

Youth in age is more pleasant than age in youth.

A person begins life as a child and ends up as a child.

If you don't find an old person in your house, go and buy yourself one.
[Arabs, and Muslims in general, believe that the presence of an old person at home brings blessings to the household.]

I am old, I don't fear death.
[Old age is not a place of weakness and fear.]

Regret not an age on the wane
That leaves behind a new one
Of a good name with good deeds
Throughout life you have won.

A person with an empty heart won't age.
['Empty heart' here refers to someone who is carefree or who has a clear conscience.]

AGGRESSION

'Take his sack and beat him,' ordained the double aggressor.

Injustice might win a round of an hour, but justice will win forever.

We make you tribes and peoples to get acquainted with each other; the best of you are those pious amongst you.
– THE QUR'AN
[Co-existence rather than aggression as a way of survival.]

ALLIES

If you eat at the prince's table you shall fight with his sword.

A

If the dog didn't count, its master should.

The alliance between the dog and its tail.

Don't send your hired hand hungry to the battlefield.

An ally of two rivals must be betraying one of them.

When the sultan is gone, gone with him are his alliances.

AMBITION

Wield your sword and become an emir, open your door and become a vizier.

Seekers of fortunes and of knowledge are two who never get their fill.

Looking upwards tires the neck.

Don't climb too high, lest you fall too deep.

If an ambitious person becomes a bridge, take the long way round.

Climb like a cucumber and fall like an eggplant/aubergine.

The eye is long, the hand is short.

Do you like pearls? Dive, then, into the sea. Do you desire a bride? Go up to her on the mount.

Driving ambitions have one end for all: a little power, then a pit for an eternal rest.

Do you want to climb the sky? It's too high. Do you want to get down to the Earth? It's under your feet already.

Paradise must be a nice place for sure, but one has to squeeze one's heart to get there.
– AFGHAN

Not every goal is attained by a trip –
Winds sometimes blow against the ship.

ANGER

Anger begins with folly and ends in repentance.

An angry man is akin to a madman.

If you want to see how big a man is, see what makes him angry.

This is not a pomegranate, but a heart full of rage.

A

A pious person's anger doesn't last longer than putting their turban right again.

The sparrow was irate with the threshing floor.
[Of displeasure with one's means of sustenance.]

Beware of the calm person's anger and the attack of a tame beast.

A wise man was asked whether anger had a remedy. 'Yes, it has,' he said, 'endure your own errors and be patient with those of others.'

Anger is a pond; once it is full up, it flows over.
– PERSIAN

The strong one is not the stalwart, but the one who can control their anger.
– HADITH

Understanding people makes you tolerate them.
– Lilminber

Of ANIMALS

Eagles are big birds, but sparrows have big hearts.
[They look nice and sing all the time.]

Barking dogs don't bite.

Don't go close to a scorpion, but you may unroll your mat near a snake.

An ant eats more than its head can take.
[Of little creatures that can perform big jobs.]

An ostrich is neither a bird nor a camel.
[When it was asked to carry something, 'I am a bird,' it said; when it was asked to fly, 'I am a camel'.]

A lion doesn't drink where a dog has licked.

A lion's den can't be empty of bones.

A peacock has a beautiful tail but an ugly voice.

Animals with nice tails may parade in their own right.

As God has not bent the top of the palm tree, He has endowed the giraffe with a long neck.

A mountain goat is healthier than a city doctor.
– KURDISH

A donkey is the poor person's horse.

Does the sparrow know what the eagles think?

A snake doesn't bite its sister.
[OR: A dog doesn't bite its tail.]

A

As timid as a dog, as obstinate as a mule and as showy as a peacock.

Treat your horse as if it were your friend; ride your horse as if it were your enemy.

Keep these mounts sound and healthy, and take care of them while idle. Have you no fear that they would complain (on Doomsday) of your mishandling of them?
– HADITH
[The Prophet Muhammad once passed by a man sharpening his knife in front of a goat. 'Afela-bila?!' ('Can't you do without it?!') he told him. He also once passed by a man sitting on his donkey and asked him not to make a seat out of the animal's back.]

ANXIETY

Woman, horse and book dispel the anxieties of the world.

A candle does not dispel the gloom of anxiety.
– ANDALUSIAN

APPEARANCE

Even a goat has a beard.
[A beard is a sign of respectability among Arabs.]

Not all those who painted their faces black are blacksmiths.

Only bones make noise in the plate.

Don't empty your water-sack at the sight of a mirage.

Don't let turbans deceive you!
[Turbans are the traditional headgear of 'all-knowing' members of the clergy. However, they are also worn by lay people.]

'Here is my turban!' said the illiterate Bahlool to a woman who had asked him to read a letter for her. He took off his turban and put it on the head of the protesting woman and told her: 'Go on, then, read it yourself!'

Not all round things are walnuts, nor all long things bananas.

An embellished face with an empty stomach.

Eat two loaves, but don't put two gowns on.

Cross a roaring river rather than a serene stream.

An impressive edifice is not necessarily a sanctuary.

Born round won't die square.
– ANDALUSIAN

Tall as a palm tree, yet with the mind of a goat.

Big nose, great character.

Bahlool at a party

Bahlool was once invited to a party. It happens that he went in shabby clothes. The host sent him away, saying that respectable guests would be offended by Bahlool's appearance. Bahlool went home, put on new garments and came back to the party. Seeing him now well-dressed, the host welcomed him in and offered him his best food. Bahlool then started to ladle food on to his sleeves to the amazement of his host. 'What on earth are you doing?!' asked the host. 'I am just feeding my garments, Sir,' responded Bahlool, 'because it is they that are the guests here.'

APPROVAL

An approving eye sees no faults, a disapproving one digs for them.

Approval is effortless. – Lilminber

Applause is the virtue of the applauder rather than the applauded.

To attain people's approval is to annoy kings.

Approval in the eyes of Bahlool

Bahlool had a disobedient son. Whenever he was asked by his father to do something he always refused, saying what would people say. Deciding to teach him a lesson, Bahlool rode his donkey and asked his son to follow him. No sooner had they gone a few paces when they passed by a woman who excalimed: 'O man! Isn't there any mercy in your heart? You ride and let the poor little boy walk behind?'

Bahlool then dismounted and asked his son to ride. They went a little further passing some elderly folk. One nudged another and said: 'Look at that fool! See how the children are being brought up these days.' Turning to Bahlool he said: 'O man! You – an old man – are walking whilst leaving the mount to this young fellow, yet you hope to educate him in the ways of life?'

'Did you hear?' said Bahlool to his son. 'Let us now both ride for a change.' In no time they came upon a group of people who shouted at them: 'Don't you even fear God? You two ride this poor creature with all your fleshy bulk that weighs more than it does.'

'Let us both walk and lead the beast behind us,' Bahlool told his son. They soon

passed some people who mocked them saying: 'Why don't you carry this donkey and relieve it from the burden of the road!' So Bahlool stopped at a tree, cut off a thick branch, tied the donkey to its middle and set off with his son, both of them raising the stick to their shoulders and carrying the poor animal. Walking together in this manner they soon attracted a crowd. Then along came the sultan's guards, who dispersed the crowd and led the two men to the madhouse. On their way there Bahlool turned to his son and said: 'Such, my son, is the end of one who does a deed in the hope of winning the approval of others.' People's approbation is an unattainable end.

ASCETICISM

No asceticism (is approved) by the faith. – HADITH

The Prophet once passed by a monk who was worshiping God in solitude and asked him who provided for him. 'My brother,' said the monk. 'It is your brother, then, who is the worshipper,' said the Prophet.

Asceticism is self-denial, greed is denial of others; to allow yourself and others their due is true virtue. – Lilminber

ASKING

Ask and receive an answer.

They who ask about the road won't go astray.

The mind echoes to a shock; the heart to a plea.

They asked and we answered; they are gone and we are ready to answer again. – IRAQI ['Answered' here implies 'responded favorably' or 'giving without stinting'.]

'Is this wheat or barley?' 'Neither,' came the answer to the awkward question.

ASSOCIATES

Your associates are your kith and kin.

Treat your superior as a father, your equal as a brother and your junior as a son.

Don't tie up the scabby (goat) near the healthy one, lest the healthy one gets scabby.

If you get along with a blacksmith, some sparks will fly out at your face.

Place a donkey near a donkey and it will learn how to bray.

A

A bird brings down a bird.

The water of the Nile loses sweetness when it mixes with the sea.

She who stays the night at the lake will be awakened by frogs.

AUTHORITY

Kindness out of season destroys authority.
– SHEIKH SADI, thirteenth century Persian Sufi poet

When a hen gives the call to prayers, slaughter it.

[It is usually the cock which performs this function at dawn.]

If the sultan smiles, he'll show tiger teeth.

If you want to be obeyed, command what is feasible.

Authority is God's shadow on earth.

Poor conduct destroys authority.

Authority is responsibility, hence few bear it well. – Lilminber

AWKWARDNESS

He stumbles over a camel.

A quiet one at the wedding!
[Wedding parties are clamorous.]

'It's a bull, sir.'
'Go and milk it then.'

The awkward one loses his right, the weak one his place.

A man was asked where his ear was. He held his right ear with his left hand from behind.

[This little joke is popular amongst Middle-Eastern peoples. City-dwellers say he is a Bedouin, Arabs say he is a Kurd, Iranians say he is an Arab.]

AXIOMS

If you fell from the heavens you would land on earth.

If you put your hand under your armpit, you'll find it right there.

One sheep, one skin.
– TURKISH

An accountant's job
The late Haj Ahmed, the illiterate Kurdish merchant of Baghdad, had a way of interviewing applicants for an accountancy job with him. 'How many are one plus one?' he asked them at the outset. All those who came out with the correct answer directly failed. As it happened, this writer took out a pencil and a piece of paper and set about tackling the simple mathematical question. He got the job right away.

B

A Bedouin took his revenge after forty years, and it was said that he was in a hurry.

BEDOUIN

He who kills a Bedouin's camel must carry his water for him.

A Bedouin's beard is his towel.
[He needs the fat stuck to his beard after the meal to soften his skin, dried up by exposure to the blazing desert sun.]

A Bedouin looks for the meal to be ready, not for it to cool off.

A Bedouin seen eating, easing his bowels and killing lice all at the same time was asked what he was doing. 'I am letting in something good, removing something bad, and killing an enemy,' he replied.

The Aba
See a Bedouin off with an 'Aba-robe' even if he were coming from the 'Aba' town.

The Aba is a traditional flowing robe mostly in black or gray, sometimes in white or gray-and-white stripes. It is usually worn to cover men from shoulders to ankles and women from top to toe. The Aba is still quite popular in some Arab countries like Iraq and in the Levant, but in some others like Saudi Arabia and the Gulf states it is worn mainly by the élite and denotes status. It is, however, a multipurpose garment quite practical for life in the rural and desert areas. It has all manner of other uses – as headgear, as a cushion for the head when carrying something weighty, saddle-sack, wall shelf, basket hanging from a tree, baby cradle or swing, rope, mat, bedding, curtain, veil, fishing net, boat sail, mask against sand storm, fire-extinguisher, improvised weapon against an attacking animal, something with which to wave SOS signals, and hand-fan.

As a gown it is capable of hiding unsightly bulges and can give one the appearance of being taller. When the Aba gets too old to be worn or for any of its other uses, it can be easily unraveled into

cont'd

The beggar and the destitute have due share in your fortunes.
– THE QUR'AN

BEHAVIOR

Beware of the noble one whom you insulted, the fool with whom you dallied, and the wanton you are taken with.

Be civil in public and gentle in private.

People have their own angels at their shoulders.
– HADITH
[In order to check their daily conduct 'in the light of God's commandments'.]

A camel doesn't eat with a spoon.

woolen yarn, or camel or goat hair (from which it was traditionally woven). This can be taken to the Aba weaver who will revive it by turning it into a new Aba. No surprise then that Arabs consider it a graceful dress and have worn it down the ages.

BEGGAR

A loaf in a beggar's hand is a wonder.

While a beggar was stretching out his hand, a cat meowed to him.

He who asks 'darkens' half of his face, he who rejects him 'darkens' his entire face.

Begging is a treasure and you don't need to enter the door.

Do not wrong the orphan, nor chide the beggar.
– THE QUR'AN

An ancient counsel on good conduct
Guard your solemnity against vanity, your rigor against haste, your punishment against injustice, your pardon against weakness, your silence against muteness, your listening against misunderstanding, your knowledge against folly, your pleasure against indecency, your leisure against waste of time, your maneuver against surrender, your love against too many demands, and your discretion against intimidation.
– IMAM ALI, seventh century, the fourth Khalif of Islam, to his governor of Egypt.

Don't do in private what you don't do in public.

Like a dancing horse, some mark time but they go nowhere (and do nothing).

If you can't be a rose, don't be a thorn. – KURDISH

B

Good counsel may be granted, but not good manners.

Good manners enrich the giver more than the recipient.
– PERSIAN

Lucman the fabulist was asked from whom he had learnt manners. 'From the unmannerly,' he replied.

Turn not your cheek in scorn toward folk, nor walk with pertness on earth. Lo! God does not love the vainglorious. Be modest in your gait and subdue your voice; the harshest of voices is the braying of the asses.
– THE QUR'AN

BENEFICENCE

Someone wondered who his real brother was:
'My father's son or the stranger?'
'The beneficent one,' came the answer.

Do good and throw it into the river.
['Later on you won't fail to get it back,' goes the advice]

BLACKMAIL

Sweets, sweets, I love sweets: fill my mouth with sweets, or else...
[...it will stay open!]

Do you take me for an apricot-tree that you would shake every now and again?
– LEVANTINE

Blackmail, when used against the innocent, is a double offense.
– Lilminber

BOASTING

The scabby-headed one boasted of her sister's hair.

Don't say: My father was... but say: Here I am.

An ounce of boasting takes away a hundredweight of virtue.
– SHEIKH SADI, thirteenth century Persian Sufi poet

BONDS

They ate bread and salt together.
[Tradition demands that if strangers eat 'bread and salt' together, ie food containing them, they would then be bound to goodwill and peace among themselves.]

To her who taught you a letter, you shall forever stay a debtor.

B

BOOK

A book is a garden that you carry in your pocket.
– SHEIKH SADI, thirteenth century Persian Sufi poet

One can learn theories better from a book, but to grasp their essence one must put them into practice.

It is the audience that makes the speaker, and the readers who write the book.

It is for its contents that one kisses the book.

The BORE

Whenever she got lost, I would come across her.
[Of an unbearable person whom one happens to meet too often.]

Your day is long and your sun persists forever.
[The hot Arabian sun is not something one desires to be exposed to for any length of time; so, too, the bore.]

A bore is as heavy a burden on himself as on others.

BOREDOM

The flame of anxiety rather than the boredom of availability.

When time grows long it feels like a snake.

The remedy for boredom is to get used to it.
– TURKISH

BOY

The work of a boy can be good, but no-one is happy about it.

A girl's tale is sweet, a boy's tale is true.

A boy is a boy even if he built a town.

BREAD

Bite my heart, not my bread.
['Bread' here implies means of livelihood.]

A person's bread is a debt.
[Owed for instance to the tiller and the baker, implying a person's inability to function in isolation.]

If you have two loaves, sell one and buy yourself a rose.
– PERSIAN

B

Roses are scented, but bread keeps us alive.

Better to open my mouth with my own bread than to close it with others'.

BRIBERY

Fill his mouth and talk to him.
[OR: Fill the mouth, and the eye will get shy.]

Put your silver up, your worries will be put down.

He who goes alone to the kadi will come back with satisfaction.
[A kadi is a judge.]

Send your silver to your bidding and stay at home.

Pay his price and curse him thrice.

The judge five cucumbers as a bribe will take, And grant ten beds of melons for their sake.
– SHEIKH SADI, thirteenth century Persian Sufi poet

BRIDE

Who is well established, who is wind, for whom shall I hold my love?
– Said by SUMERIAN women of marriageable age

If her household praise her, leave her; if her neighbors praise her, take her and run away with her.

A bride from Persia: for every step she is worth a town.
[To neighboring Arabs, Persian women are renowned for their charm and beauty.]

A bride in summer and a baby in winter are a ready blessing from the Giver.

First year, a bride; second year, a spy; third year a seven-headed snake.
[In-laws' talk in Aleppo, Syria, when a bride started her married life living with them.]

No sooner had he smelled under her armpit than he forgot about his kindred.

15

C

> Can one have a baby without conceiving, can one get fat without eating?
> – SUMERIAN

CAREFREE

I don't have a donkey, I don't fear the rock.

Her bread is baked and her water is (already) in the jar.

CAUSE

The donkey slipped because of the 'monkey'.
[That is, its rider.]

A loaf is as big as the dough.

The fire will burn only the foot treading on it.

How can the shadow be straight when the stick is crooked?

He whose molar aches keeps talking about it.

If you want to save the peach, kill the worm.

Look at the grain of pepper and the size of the sneeze.

If you withhold firewood from the fire, it will stop burning.

No marriage without consent, no exertion without sweat.
– SUMERIAN

Although God is all-powerful, he won't send down rain from a clear sky.
– AFGHAN

A nail may save the horse, the horse may save the rider, and the rider may save the land.
– PERSIAN

Causes are diverse but death is one.

A mark points to a marker and dung points to a camel.
[Bedouin proof of God's existence.]

One can't eat a nut before breaking it.

There are doors in heavens and pathways on earth.
[It is counseled in the Qur'an that the livelihoods of the faithful are allotted for them in heaven, but the paths by which they can be attained are already on earth.]

C

A story goes that a Bedouin entered the Prophet's mosque, leaving his camel untied outside. When he was told to go and tie it up, he came up to the Prophet saying that he only trusted it to God, therefore he had set it free.

'Go and tie it up (first), then trust it to God, O son of the Arabs,' replied the Prophet.

CHANGE

O God, spare us the winds of change.

If you raised your hands from prayers with your heart changed, your prayers would be answered.

Change yourself and your luck will change too.
– TURKISH

Allah will not change the state of a folk until they change what is in their hearts.
– THE QUR'AN

CHARACTER

Hammer water, it will remain water.

Don't blame your mother for your character.

You are the child of seven generations.

A snake brings forth only a snake.

The fine pullet shows its excellence right from the egg.

A horse is a horse, whether it runs or trots.

A crab was asked why it walked sideways. 'This is the way I like to walk,' it said.

We are easy to swallow but hard to digest.
– LEVANTINE

Only what is there may ooze from a sack.

The falcon dies while its eyes are fixed on the prey.

CHARITY

Charity banishes evil.

Don't be charitable when you are yourself in need.

Charity is not innocent, for poverty is the twin of luxury. – Lilminber

CHILDREN

Conceiving a child is pride, giving birth is pain, yet raising it is the job.

When a child falls silent, grievance follows.

If you were not mad when you married, you would be when you had to rock the cradle.

With them there's worry, and without them there's worry.

He came out of the egg and spat on it.
[Of an ungrateful child.]

'Whom would you care for most?' a Bedouin mother was asked. 'The little one until she is grown-up, the sick one until he is healed, and the absent one until he is back home,' she said.

Eat with the mother of a child, but don't travel with her.
[This is not really advice against traveling with a mother and her child as such, but a reminder of the responsibility that comes along with it.]

The children's kadi hung himself.
[Apparently because he got mixed up in their quarrels and could not possibly settle them. A kadi is a judge.]

A boy is a boy, even if he built a town.

We put our daughter in a locker, (yet) her news filled up the marketplace.
['She set herself free looking at large for her destiny' – against limiting the personal freedom of daughters.]

Fathers ate sour grapes, and their sons suffer toothache.
[Sons have to bear the mistakes or sins of their fathers.]

Bring up your son as a child and befriend him as a man.

A child needs a whole village to take care of her.
– SUDANESE

Children are like the spots of a carpet: each one has a different shade.

Children send evil away.
[Parents would be too busy taking care of them to engage in household arguments.]

CHOICE

Good things make choosing difficult, bad things leave no choice.

Your choice shows what you are.

When brought to the gallows, the choosy one asked to be hanged with a gaudy rope.

CLEANLINESS

Cleanse your floor if you don't know who trod on it, and wash your face if you don't know who kissed it.

Even washing one's mouth with one's tongue is cleanliness.
A man who likes to stay clean will clean his things by himself.

God loves the clean.
– THE QUR'AN

CLEVERNESS

The lucky need not be clever, yet the clever need luck.

O my child, don't be clever, just be good.

CLIMATE

When roses bloom in May, sit in the shade and remember the frost.
– LEBANESE

Winter is narrow even if it is large.
['Narrow' here implies restrictive to movement.]

What is killed by the sun won't be revived by water; what is killed by water won't be revived by the sun.

COMMONALITY

Put your head together with other heads and pray for safety.

We went to the kadi to complain, the kadi began weeping with us.
[A kadi is a judge.]

In prayers and in prison all people are equal.

COMPANY

Hearts are streams – if they meet they make rivers.

Harmony is the soul of companionship.

Solitude is better than bad company.

The lane is narrow, and everyone knows their own company.
[The 'lane', used here to denote social circles, is not that wide and so everybody knows their own position and associates in the community.]

Live with them for forty days, either you become one of them or you had better leave them.

Eat bitter, drink bitter, but don't live with the bitter one.

Long companionship reveals character.

Show me your company, and I'll show you what you are.

Seek a comrade for the road and a neighbor for the house.

Don't go on the road with a boy: if your donkey falls he'll laugh at you, and if his donkey falls he'll come weeping to you.

If you don't stay with me you'll be alone, and if I don't stay with you I'll be lonely.

No road is too long with good company.

One man drove the donkey, another sang for it.

You who are like us, come to us!

Solitude in safety is better than association with repentance.

Good company is a feast.

They that sleep near the pond will have frogs for companions.

If you see two in harmony, the one must be bearing the other.

COMPASSION

Have mercy on those below you, so that the One above you may have mercy on you.

Lighten the load of the donkey and so get it off your own chest.

Neither has he mercy on me, nor does he let others' mercy reach me, nor does he let God's mercy come down on me!

God is more merciful than his creatures.

Only the merciful will merit God's mercy.
– HADITH

COMPETENCE

A rider of two camels would split in two.

Give the bread to its baker even if she would eat half of it.
['Bread' alludes here to the dough ready to be baked, but metaphorically also to the task at hand.]

Don't offer to show the muleteer the way to the market place!

I had beaten those with several pursuits, but the one with a singular pursuit beat me.
– SHEIKH HUSSAIN BAHAA'I AL-AMILY, seventeenth century scholar who wrote on every branch of knowledge known to Islamic culture at the time

COMPETITION

At the race the winning horse will be known.

The one who is ahead of you by one step is ahead of you the whole way long.

The winning edge is thin as a thread.

Traders only rub shoulders so that they can hold the market together.

COMPLAINT

Complain to the bow, and it will send you an arrow.

The donkey suffered the burden, and the tick cried out.

Don't complain to the eagle, for it looks out for the wounded.

Talk to a friend, demand from a rival but don't complain to a foe.
– PERSIAN

Complain in vain and you'll cause pain.

CONFESSION

Confession of a sin merits half-forgiveness.

One's confession is one's own verdict.

CONFORMITY

If you come to a town that worships a calf, cut grass and feed it.
[The Arabic variant of 'When in Rome...']

C

If the mountain doesn't come to you, go to the mountain.

Rather wrong with everyone than right on your own.

If the whole mob hauls, turn and haul with it.

Be a crook with the crooked and with the one-eyed shut one eye.

Do as your neighbors, or keep your door shut.

CONSCIENCE

Have a good conscience and fear no evil.
[OR: Godly is our conscience when it is clear.]

Conscience is the judge from whose verdict one can't escape.

Conscience is a just but weak executor.
– ANDALUSIAN

You can wash your gown but not your conscience.

CONSIDERATION

The sun shines for people, not for itself.

Put your finger in your eyes and guess how much it would hurt others.

See with others' eyes, and they will see with yours.

CONTENTMENT

Whoever possesses much silver may be happy, whoever possesses much barley may be happy, but whoever has naught can sleep.
– SUMERIAN

'Take it for nothing!'
'Sorry, I have no place for it.'

A wise person was asked: Who is contented? 'The one who does not look for what is not there until there is no more of what is there,' was the reply.

C

Contentment is an inexhaustible treasure.

Everyone is content with their mind; no-one is content with their lot.

Stretch your feet but only up to your bedcover.

Done by consent makes content.

CONTRASTS

I hear rumbling but can't see grinding.
[Of ostensibly being busy doing something without a tangible result.]

As tall as a palm-tree but with the mind of a goat.

The pilgrim trading in rosaries!
[Pilgrimage is a holy duty whilst trading is a material pursuit – mixing the two brings the pilgrim's piety into question.]

Go up the tree and pick figs – come down the fig tree, who told you to go up there?!

CONVENIENCE

Every convenience brings its own inconvenience.

Convenience is like shallow water: you can wet yourself with ease, but you can't swim in it. The mature swimmer seek the depths for fulfillment.
– Lilminber

Convenience is not contentment, but contentment is convenient.
– Lilminber

COOK

The pots are empty and the cook is content.

The cook needs wooden legs and an iron tongue.

Too many cooks will burn the pot.

Cooking is the art of keeping an eye on the fire.

Not everyone who blew was a cook.

A cook recognizes the face of a hungry person.

She is cooking couscous with rabbit whilst the rabbit is still in the woods.

CO-OPERATION

Hand over hand will reach the sky.

Mutual help and co-operation are like praying and adoration.

Two in harmony can take a town.

C

CORRUPTION

Fish begin to stink at the head.

He who is caught between the onion and its peel will pick up the stink.
[Don't take up with the corrupt.]

The market of debauchery is always open.

Rather live in the land of corruption than in the land of vicious envy.

COUNSEL

Take advice from the one who arrived a night before you.

Give counsel to your friend, let it be sweet or bitter.

Take counsel (even) from the head of an ox.

Giving advice in public is a reproach and in private is instruction.

Follow the one who made you weep, not the one who made you laugh.

May God bless her who showed my faults to me!

Give counsel to a fool and gain a foe.

Give your counsel to a thousand and your secret to none.

'O people, let me hear your counsel, for I make no decision without your consent.'
– THE QUEEN OF SHEBA in THE QUR'AN

No right judgment without counsel.

COURAGE

Calamity is the touchstone of brave minds.

To be courageous is not to be fearless, but to go ahead despite fear.
– TURKISH

Courage is facing one's weaknesses.

COWARDICE

Coward's mother need not worry.
[The coward doesn't take risks.]

A coward looks backwards whilst death bears down on him from above.

Afraid of the shadow of her ears.

Every cock crows on its own dunghill.

If you want to know who is the bravest coward, it is the one who first dares to kick the fallen lion.

The rule of a coward... ('is destructive and mean.')

And when a coward felt safe and alone,
He challenged a thousand knights on his own.

CREEDS

Eat with Jews, sleep among Christians and buy from Muslims.
['Jews cook and eat well, Christians are supposedly peaceful, and Muslims are 'God-fearing' in trade.']

Creeds disperse; knowledge unites.
– KING OGLO OF TASHKENT

Creeds are tribal, faith is universal.

The Exalted Stars, some say, do also feel,
Just like us, and think and talk too;
For Heaven's sake, do they also have creeds
That would brand us Muslim, Christian
                              and Jew?
– ABUL ALAA AL-MA'ARRI, eleventh century poet

God helps everyone according to one's own creed.

CRITICISM

The camel never sees its own hump, but that of another.

The net said to the sieve: 'Your eyes are small.'

When a plate is broken at the hands of the mistress of the house, no one will hear a sound.

A shrewd critic weighs in an accurate scale.
– IBN KHALDOON, fourteenth century historian

CUNNING

He takes you to the river and brings you back thirsty.

If you lunch on a ruse, you won't dine on it.

There must be a fox in every wood.

The fox sleeps with its tail on the hen house.

If you're a fox, I'm your tail!
[I'm as cunning.]

What the rat can't reach with its tongue it'll take with its tail.

Honey can lure the snake out of its hole.

He lived on cunning and died of hunger.

CURSE

Curse the Sultan in his absence and Satan in his presence.

Nations curse one another, although they come from one father and one mother.

Don't launch arrows of curses at your enemy, lest you hit your friend.

CUSTOMS

Customs are the fifth element of the world.
[After water, air, earth and fire.]

Customs are a plague to the wise and the idols of fools.

Customs are a candle carried by a blind person in front of the blindfolded.
– ANDALUSIAN

Customs are accentuated habits.

D

Every day of your life is a page in your history.
– SHEIKH SADI, thirteenth century Persian Sufi poet

DAYS

If you miss one day, take another.

Don't thank a day before it has come to an end, nor praise a woman before she is a grandmother.

When you are covered by days you are rendered naked. ['Covered' here implies 'overcome'.]

If daylight fails you, counter it with bonfire.

His day is his heyday.

Our days are a serpent in
    black and white
Gripping us tightly for its
    mortal bite;
We love to live on just for
    fear of decease:
In false hope we strive – in
    despair we fight.
– ABUL ALAA AL-MA'ARRI,
eleventh century poet

Days are but brothers – sons of one parent,
And a night is but a sister of a night;
Ask not of one what the other has not given.
– ABUL ALAA AL- MA'ARRI

'Tis all a Chequer-board of nights and days,
Where Destiny with Men for Pieces plays;
Hither and thither moves, and mates,
             and plays,
And one by one back in the closet lays.
– OMAR KHAYYAM (1048 - 1131), Persian mathematician, astronomer and poet

DANCING

When a dancer repents, her shoulders keep on shaking.

Dancing starts with prancing.

Don't marry a dancer, even if she is a tailor.
– EGYPTIAN

He who doesn't know how to dance says the ground is uneven.

DAY OF JUDGMENT

Give your gold and silver away, before your forehead is burnt with them on Doomsday.
– HADITH

Those who promise and won't perform will be brought on Doomsday near the door of Paradise for it to be shut in their faces.
– HADITH

Bahlool was asked when Doomsday would come. 'The day I die,' he replied.

DEAR ONES

A dear one asking for not such a dear thing. – IRAQI
[An expression of endearment common amongst close friends, when one of them asks for a favor or service that would be granted with pleasure.]

If the captain likes you, you may wipe your hands on the sail.

The dead one is the dearest one in the family.

DEATH

There is but one way to enter life, but the exit gates are without number.

A boat stranded for a hundred years may float again; love and death are trips without return.

God made us equal only in death.

Death is but of one kind.

Let him go home whose 'oil is exhausted'.

Die bravely for you will die but once.

When the ant grows wings it will fly to its grave.

'Do you want to die by hanging or by strangling?' asked the hangman.

Death is a black camel kneeling at everyone's door in turn.

D

A thousand miserable lives rather than sleeping under a stone.
[Preferring misery to death.]

If you don't want to die, you won't see those who died before you.

The graveyard and the miser take, yet give nothing in return.

The Angel of Death is blind.
[Presumably, because it often also takes away the souls of those who still deserve to live.]

Why are you so afraid of death? Don't you often long for a long deep sleep?
– KAHLIL GIBRAN (1833 - 1931), Lebanese mystical writer, poet and artist

However high you raise your castle to the sky, you will be buried down in the earth.

Don't torment the dead in their graves.
[Keep them in your good memories.]

O my soul, don't die – summertime is ushered in, and together with it will come the sugar beets!
– LEVANTINE

Death is our eternal host.

The one who dies for a cause will be remembered by it.

A man is born crying whilst people laugh around him; let him die laughing whilst people cry around him.
– PERSIAN

Praise a day in the evening and a person at the end of their line.

A slaughtered goat won't be bothered by flaying.

One can't stare into the sun, nor into death.

Do you need counsel? Forget about death while you still live.

My father died and was healed of his fever.
– AFGHAN

Each soul tastes death before its death.

We are the children of the dead, and shall drink from their cup.

She was thrown into a night which had no sister.

When a rich man dies, his bottom exudes honey.

He who kills himself is not to be mourned.

In prison and death all people are equal.

Our souls are but hired, and what is hired must be given back.

Death does not build a bridge.
[Only life can do that.]

D

When a man dies, those who survive him ask what he has left behind; the Angel who bends over the dying man asks what good deeds he has sent out before him.
– HADITH

DEBT

Debt is humiliation in daytime, and worry at night.

The debtor will reap no harvest.

Take and ask for more (from a bad debtor).
[OR: Take even a stone from a bad debtor.]

The one who owes you a span owes me a cubit.

No credit, no reproach, and God caters for all.
[Often displayed on signboards in front of shops.]

Be not in debt to a rich person nor let someone poor be indebted to you.

Give credit and lose your money; ask for repayment and get an enemy.

O, honorable count, we must some day settle the account.

Don't sell grain to a bird on credit.

A thousand tears won't repay a debt.
– TURKISH

She who has wheat can borrow some flour.

He who has taken and given back is not to be denied a deal.

No debtor was ever hanged.
– IRAQI
[This refers to Iraq's prosperity.]

An aristocrat stays indebted for his loaf of bread to the one who gave it to him.

DEEDS

Deeds are to be judged by intentions.

Judge a person, not by what they say but by what they do.

D

Good deeds cut off the tongues of gossip.

We are at a loss, O scabby-headed one, where
we should kiss you!
[Male strangers greet women with a kiss on the head.
The essence of this exclamation is that someone's
record of ill-deeds left others with no desire to meet
them with good cheer.]

Do good and throw it into the river.
[OR: Whatever you do, you will find it ahead of you.]

Deeds remain gaudy, if not cooked on the fire of
sincerity.
– Lilminber

She whose origins are lost, look at her deeds.
[That is, in order to judge someone unknown to you
observe the sort of things they do.]

Show them your deeds, not your genealogy.
– HADITH

DELAY

Good is the delay that makes sure.

What is deferred is not abandoned.

DEMANDS

A well partakes of many a rope.

Every day shake off your dates, O my good
palm-tree!
[Of demanding too much too often.]

The calf opens its mouth from afar (once it
spots its mother).

Demand a right and request a good turn.

Request from a stranger, ask from a friend
and demand from a rival.

DESIRE

Desires are the throbs of lively souls.
– PERSIAN

The dearest thing to the heart is that which
is forbidden.

And it may be that you desire a thing that
bears but evil for you.
– THE QUR'AN

Life is nothing but a wish and the will to
accomplish it.
– Lilminber

Ah Love! Could you and I with Fate conspire
To grasp this sorry scheme of things entire;
Would not we shatter it to bits – and then
Remold it nearer to the Heart's Desire!
– OMAR KHAYYAM (1048 - 1131), Persian
mathematician, astronomer and poet

31

D

DESPAIR

A cornered snake bites its belly.

DESTINY

I am a thoroughbred steed, but I am hitched to a mule, and must draw a cart and carry reeds and stubble.
– SUMERIAN

He ran from the bear and fell into the well.

Wherever it is sown, wheat always goes to the millstone.

She zigzagged to Paradise, lest she would go straight to Hell.

The path of destiny has many a crossroads.

The camel wanted to go one way, and its rider another; yet God's will ruled over both.

Destiny favors the few and harasses the many.
– PERSIAN

The strongest of men will fall to fate if he has no judgment.
– SUMERIAN

DEVIL

The devil knows his God, but still tries to cheat him.

The devil knows more than people, because he is much older.
– PERSIAN

An ardent devil is better than an inept angel.

Doing a good turn to a villain is like lighting a candle to the devil.

The devil won't demolish his own house.

Everyone carries their own devil under their own armpit.

DILEMMA

Lament if it rains and lament if it doesn't.

If we spit upwards it will land on our mustaches. If we spit downwards it will land on our beards.
[ALSO: If I sink I'll be eaten by fish, and if I float I'll be picked at by birds.]

Don't throw yourself into the fire to escape the smoke.
– TURKISH

Dad is in love, Mum is jealous, my sister has a headache, and I stand baffled between them.

D

Let me go else I cry, hold me fast lest I fall.

DIRE STRAITS

She fled from the leak and came under the spout.

From bad to worse? Despair ye not:
There's ever an untier for every knot.

DISCIPLINE

Go in turn, not by jostling!
[When waiting, queue up.]

He whose place is not orderly and neat, his barley will eat up his wheat.

'Stand in two rows, please!'
'But we are just the two of us, Sir!'

DISCRETION

The eye sees from behind the veil.

A covered sin is two-thirds forgiven.

What you can't see with your eyes, you'll see with your mind.

Be like the ear of the measurer and his eyes.
[His ear is closed to the noise of the market place and with his eyes he sees only the crops he weighs in the warehouse. A counsel to mind one's own business.]

It is not fitting that I tell thee more,
For the stream's bed cannot hold the sea.
– SHEIKH SADI, thirteenth century Persian Sufi poet

DISGUISE

You can't hide a lance under your armpit.

It's the same donkey, only the packsaddle has changed.

Camel-riding, love and a wise person's blunder can't be hidden.

She sold her lamp to buy a curtain.

Disguise in your heart and it will slip on your tongue and wink on your eyes.

DISHARMONY

Iron struck iron and it rang.

If you are bored take some lemon, if sad resort to your tobacco pouch and pipe, and if not in harmony leave the place.

They used to be like a face and mirror, now they are the talk of the town.

No intact wall was left between them.

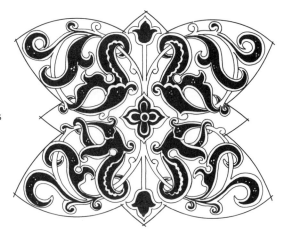

DISHONESTY

He lived by deceit and died in poverty.

Face-to-face (she is) a mirror; from behind, a thorn.

Shame on you for cheating me once, shame on me for being cheated twice.

DISLIKE

One liked him as much as one liked a leech.

I like you, I cover your faults; I dislike you, I expose them.

I am sick because of you, and you visit me in my illness?!

If you dislike someone, don't deny their due right.

DISTINCTION

A known face in an unknown place.

The duck is a cousin of the swan, yet duck is duck and swan is swan.

A sieve can't hide the sun.

An archer is distinguished not by his sharp arrows but by his score.
– PERSIAN

DIVORCE

The Seven Heavens will tremble when some one of you contemplates divorcing his wife.
– HADITH

A woman must be retained in honor or allowed to leave with kindness.
– THE QUR'AN

They who help with divorce won't help with alimony.

DRESS

A borrowed dress doesn't fit.

Wear a gown, don't let it wear you.
[Wear clothes you are comfortable in, rather than just to be fashionable.]

Eat as you please, and dress as others please.

DRINKING

A drunk won't count the glasses.

Just leave the drunk alone to fall on their own.

There are benefits in it, but its harm is greater.
– THE QUR'AN on wine.

E

Not all who toiled earned, but all who earned toiled.

Spread out on Earth and earn your living on it.
– THE QUR'AN

EDUCATION

Bring up your children other than the way you were brought up yourselves, for they were born for times other than yours.
– IMAM ALI, seventh century, the fourth Khalif of Islam

Raise your son seven years, educate him seven years, befriend him seven years, and then put his rope on his shoulder and send him to the market place.

The best horse needs breaking and the best child needs education.

EARNING

Earn a penny a day, but don't be idle.

The dog bought it and the dog ate it.

Moving around leads to gain.

Toil first, and then play.

Don't spend money before you earn it.

Earning your daily bread is the greater jihad.
– HADITH
['Jihad' or 'striving' is a religious duty to promote the faith and ensure its application by the faithful in their worldly dealings.]

Learned in youth is engraved in stone.

A man in his manhood is the result of how his mother brought him up in his childhood.
– QASIM AMEEN, Egyptian writer

Let your child shout but don't shout at it.
– BEDOUIN

EFFECT

A brand only burns the spot it falls upon.

Throw a stone at the wall and it will leave a mark on it.

A receptacle of oil oozes oil, and a vessel of vinegar seeps vinegar.

END

To every beginning there is an end.

The worst day for a rooster is when its feet are washed.

When the end draws near, the eyes will glaze over.

When my intestines poured out I gave them to my cat.
– TURKISH

The real defects of work will only show when it is finished.

If you want to drown, why should it be in clear water?
– PERSIAN

The one to be hanged may call their hangman names.

One thing is certain and the rest is lies;
The Flower that once has blown forever dies.
– OMAR KHAYYAM (1048 – 1131), Persian mathematician, astronomer and poet

ENEMY

A thousand friends can't undo the harm of one enemy.

She who hated you last year can't love you this year.

A serpent can't be a sister, nor can an enemy be a friend.

Eat a bucket of salt in front of an enemy.
[Don't show them your soft spot.]

Ally with the strong and dodge your enemies.

The saliva of an enemy is a murderous poison.

I didn't see a warm evening in wintertime, nor a clear heart in an enemy.

Take your enemy as a snake, even if he were a rope.

Rivers can sleep but an enemy can't.

Beware of cooking meat twice and of a reconciled enemy.

Pass by an enemy while you are hungry, never while you are naked.

Don't run so fast after a fleeing enemy.

Trust no new friend, nor an old enemy.

E

A needle's eye is wide enough for two friends, and the whole world is too narrow for two enemies.
– SHEIKH SADI, thirteenth century Persian Sufi poet

Don't let an enemy fix your arrow.

Four things, a little of which is too much: fire, anger, poverty and enmity.

Whenever your enemy gets mad, strike!

Rather a hundred enemies outside the house than one inside.

When your enemy starts to speak a 'foreign language', know the evil is gone.

A harmless enemy is better than a harmful friend.
[OR: A wise enemy is better than a foolish friend.]

Better to quarrel with a friend than to support an enemy.

Don't shoot arrows of curses at your enemy, lest you hit a friend.

In my foe's death, what joy is there for me?
For my life, too, cannot eternal be.
– SHEIKH SADI, thirteenth century Persian Sufi poet

What is an enemy? They are the ones we never think of having some patience to show them how to understand, appreciate and respect us.
– Lilminber

ENVY

Envy is the ax of the body.

Envy is a bone: if it sticks in your throat it will kill you.

Rather live in a land of corruption, than in a land of envy.

The envious and the hatred-ridden have but black days and white nights.
['White nights' imply sleepless ones.]

Where envy ended up who knows, it surely started with its ill-wisher and killed her.
– PERSIAN

Counting another's good fortune won't enlarge yours in any way.

A tongue of praise is an eye of envy.

Let is suffice that the envious one becomes sad when you are glad.
– KHALIF OTHMAN, seventh century, the third Khalif of Islam

EQUALITY

She who equates you with herself is your equal.

The camels of the Sultan are also unshod.

We are all the children of nine months.

Your fingers aren't equal!

Men are born equals, like the teeth of a comb.
– HADITH

ERROR

A fool's error is a red herring, a wise person's slip is a big fish.

He who does not put his error right will commit it twice.

We commit errors because we are hasty, we learn from them because we are wise.

Infallible are only the angels because they live in Heaven.

A hidden truth is better than a renowned fallacy.

Had errors a mother, it would be routine.
– AFGHAN

No one is always mistaken, even a broken clock is correct twice a day.
– TURKISH

Too much talking, too many errors.
– PERSIAN

A wise person's error is more instructive than a fool's truth.

Errors cannot but give birth to errors.
– PERSIAN

An error can't put another error right.

Error floats, truth lies down in the deep.
– PERSIAN

ESCAPE

For breaking free and eating, one does not need an invitation.

A snake which finds two holes will escape easily.

He left nothing behind him but dust.

ESTEEM

She who respects others will merit their respect.

Help those with heavy burdens and esteem them.

Self-respect is the starting-point of respecting others.

Esteem finds love, but love doesn't always find esteem.

EVENTS

Count the waves of the sea! Events to come are many more.

Events are not over while their aftermath persists.

Each length has a width, and each object a shadow.

The death of a poor person and a rich person's vice go unnoticed.

People go after their business while hazards make events.

Before the downpour I was showered with a drizzle.

Like waves of the sea, events have two sides: either you ride them out or they ride you down.

'I saw him falling!' said one.
'Before you I saw him staggering,' said the other.

Events are the teachers of fools and the wise alike.

May God save us from fire, drowning and dying on the side of the street.

EVIL

A spark can burn a town.

A person can run away from another, but not from their evil deeds.

Push evil away with evil if you can't push it with good.

A day was over but not its evil.

When the devils disappear, the angels take leave.

If one is used to evil ways, one will readily suspect the rest of the world.

The key to a stomach is a mouthful and the key to evil is a word.

Avoid evil ways, my child, and evil will avoid you.

To destroy the cobweb, destroy the spider.

E

Even if villains are musk, pierce your pocket and throw them away.

How many a person in need turned to an evil deed!

To contemplate evil is evil of itself.

Evil comes in a mass and goes in bits and pieces.
– PERSIAN

They that sow evil will reap remorse.

Do good and it will be forgotten, do evil and it will be remembered.

Harmful weeds don't die.

Push evil away with a stick, lest you have to push it with a pole.

To overcome evil with good is good, to resist evil with evil is evil.
– HADITH

He who does an atom of good will see it, and he who does an atom of evil will see it.
– THE QUR'AN

EXAGGERATION

He sees a dome in a grain and a camel in a bug.

Exaggeration is to draw a snake with legs added on.
– PERSIAN

EXCUSE

He who didn't want to lend his rope said: 'I want to hang my grain on it.'

The absent one carries his excuse with him.

To repeat an excuse is to remind of the fault.

She who warned you has absolved herself from the consequences.

He who wants to act will find the means, he who doesn't will find an excuse.

Show your excuse not your misery.

A camel went lame because of its ear.

Don't make your excuse worse than your blunder.
– PERSIAN

EXPECTATION

The fox is not yet caught, yet you are making a neck-stock for it.
– SUMERIAN

E

The early barley will flourish – how shall we know? The late barley will flourish – how shall we know?
– SUMERIAN

Anticipate good, and you'll find good.

Don't build a manger before buying the mule.

An estimate in the field was not true on the threshing floor.

O new year behind the door, come in with better luck than before.

We were looking for a drop from a cloud.
[Of having but little hope.]

What could we expect from you, O quince – a choke with every bite?

EXPERIENCE

Ask an experienced person, not a learned one.

 Learn from others' experiences, lest others would learn from yours.

Once snared and broken free, a fox is ever ready to flee.

They who are not ruled by the rudder will be ruled by the rock.

The tongue of experience is the most truthful.

The duck's first dive into the water – tail first.
– PERSIAN

One person's misfortune is another's instruction.

She who searches for knowledge must go far and wide; she who looks for experience must draw near.

He who hasn't slept on the rock of exile cannot appreciate the mat in his hut.

He who was burned by milk will blow at yogurt.
– TURKISH

A slave can't have happy dreams.

She was asked how she had learnt it; 'I did it,' she said.

EXPLOITATION

One's beard is burning, another is baking their cake on it.

Ten weavers are steady at the looms, yet the renown belongs to the 'House'.

The miller takes by the handful, the landlord by mule-loads.

The surgeon who practiced with the heads of orphans.

Away with pottage when the hen lays golden eggs.

EXTREMES

Either lighting two candles, or staying in the dark.

A ship without a captain will sink; a ship with two captains will sink, too.

Do not hold your hand in a fist to your chest, nor stretch it out too long.
– THE QUR'AN

EXUBERANCE

The sea doesn't buy fish.
– TURKISH

He has good things to eat and drink, yet he is good for nothing.

Why should those with cooks burn their own fingers?

Unearned abundance is like desert sand: it comes with the wind and goes with the wind.

Abundance is not a cause for complaint but a cause for anxiety.
– PERSIAN

Too much honey takes away its taste.

If you dip your hand in oil, rub it on the one next to you.
[Oil was a symbol of prosperity and well-being in the Levant.]

If God bestows you with plenty, beware of Him.

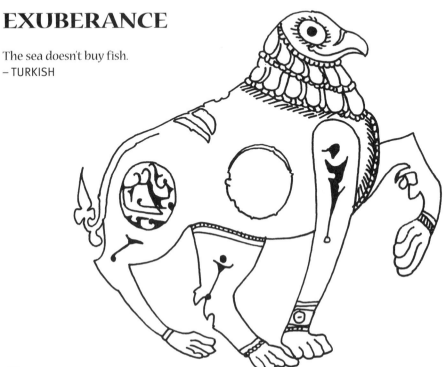

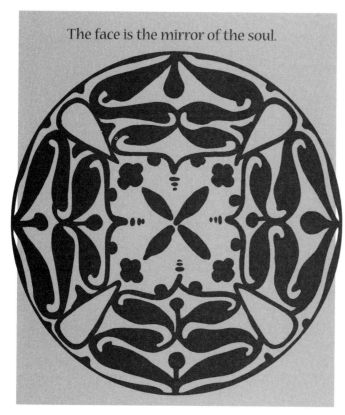

The face is the mirror of the soul.

For forty years I stood at the door of Paradise, then as I got drowsy, it opened and shut.
– SHEIKH SADI, thirteenth century Persian Sufi poet

When the camel stumbles, many a knife will go for it.

'I am fasting today,' said the cat when it saw the meat hung too high from the ceiling.

FAME

Fame will not come to you whilst you lie on a bed of feathers.

Even when fallen, a rose keeps wafting its fragrance.

A good name is better than a good face.
– SHEIKH SADI, thirteenth century Persian Sufi poet

Many stars were extinguished epochs ago, but their light is still radiating at us.
– KAHLIL GIBRAN (1883 - 1931), Lebanese mystical writer, poet and artist

FACE

A person's face is an open book if one can read it.

Your age is on your face.

He is like lentils: neither a face nor a back.
[He is without distinction or personality.]

FAMILIARITY

He delouses his camel every day and counts its hair by the way.

The nearby church doesn't heal.
[OR: A local singer doesn't charm. ALSO: The reed-player from one's own street doesn't fascinate. – PHARAONIC EGYPTIAN]

FAILURE

Of success one learns less than of failure.
No one might fail but those who try to win.
Each stumble is still an onward step.

Failure of purpose is the hardest failure.

F

FAMILY

Many hands in the field for many mouths at the table.
– SUMERIAN

It takes three to form a family.
– KURDISH

Your family may chew you, yet they won't swallow you.

Strolling with flowing sleeves in the thoroughfare, yet he was a gloomy one at home.

Without a child one has a pierced heart, but with children one has a heart like a sieve.

FARMING

Under every stone there is a loaf.

A contented peasant is a sultan little known.

The days of sowing are short and hasty, it takes time to reach the harvest.
– LEVANTINE

Were it not for the scorpions, all men would be farmers, and all maidens would remain slim (in the fields).
– Nomadic saying.

Still frail and weak, the little sapling was flooded by a creek.
[This saying also counsels against over-feeding a little baby, or caring too much for a new acquaintance or friend.]

Seeds sown in a salty lake won't yield barley to grind and bake.

Whilst roots are in the ground, people anticipate the fruit.
– PERSIAN

Hadith on cultivating the earth
The hadith, or the traditions, of the Prophet Muhammad, are the second main source of guidance for Muslims, after the Qur'an.

Take care of the Earth, she is your mother.

Plow your field and provide for your household.

Honor your aunt, the date-palm.
[It yields tasty fruit in abundance.]

Search (for) your livelihood in the treasure of the earth.

Tilling is (as sacred as) worship.

FASTING

Let her fast and pray who has no bread for her day!
[An ironic observation on fasting by the poor.]

F

Fast and pray, yet misfortune will befall you anyway.
– LEVANTINE

FAULT

His tongue was silent on his own faults.

She started the fire, then cried: 'O, God, help me!'

One's faults are not shameful, but to remind someone of a redressed fault is.

It may be that someone is blamed for no fault.

Someone scorned a pious scholar who then said: 'May God forgive my sin which justified your affront of me!'

Where the goat has a fault, the sheep is called 'Your Majesty'.

Real faults appear only when a thing is finished.

The acquiescent eye is but on faults closed,

The eye of displeasure renders them exposed.
– SHEIKH SADI, thirteenth century Persian Sufi poet

They who the faults of others bring to you,
Be sure they'll bear to others your faults too.
– SHEIKH SADI

FAVORS

Favors cut off tongues.

Favors are treasures: take care with whom you deposit them.

Bread given to a beggar is alms, otherwise it remains a debt.

He who gives you a rope will tie you down with it.
– SHEIKH SADI, thirteenth century Persian Sufi poet

One who demands is unpopular even if she is a darling.

F

May God bless him not who, granted a favor, is ungrateful, nor him who, granting one, makes it known.
– HADITH

Favors are as big as their doers.

Don't ask for a favor if you don't need it.

FEAR

Fear sees in the dark.

Don't fear God, but fear the one who doesn't fear Him.

He who doesn't know fear can't make others fear him.

She who doesn't fear Moses's stick must fear Pharoah's.

He fears the shadow of his own ears.

If you fear something face it, as standing in awe of it is more painful.

If you fear don't say, if you say don't fear.

The donkey was branded, the mule neighed and shied away.

That which you preserve with fear is the dearest; that which you preserve with valor will last longer.

Frighten the beast before the beast frightens you.

The wet one fears no rain.

Hate while you fear!
– TURKISH

Fear is the conscience of the weak.

People know courage through fear.

FEAST

The party started with a rose and ended with remorse.

The tamborine burnt up and the party-goers dispersed.

The feast broke the fasting.

Good health is a feast.

FIDELITY

Reap fidelity from the tree of confidence.

Confidence is built either in a moment of

F

trust or else in a decade of dealing. Your ability to trust is more virtuous than being trusted.
– Lilminber

FIGHT

Don't go to a fight nor gather stones for fighters.

Don't go to a fight where you were once beaten.

A dog facing two dogs is a coward, a dog facing three is dead.

It takes two to have a fight, just one to avoid it.
– Lilminber

FIRE

Fire is winter's dessert.

Fire can't be satiated with firewood.

If light fails you, resort to fire.

He who sets his house on fire will warm himself on it but once.

In the ashes I see fire, and warfare ever starts with a spark.

FIRMNESS

If its place is to be taken, a heavy rock is hard to be shaken.

Two mortals are firm in their stand: the one who knows and knows she knows, and the one who doesn't want to know what she doesn't know.

Fools and the wise won't change their minds.
– PERSIAN

FLATTERY

Don't praise the beginning before you see the end.

A toady fawned upon Imam Ali with undue flattery. 'I am under what you say and above what you think,' retorted Imam Ali.
[Imam Ali was the fourth Khalif of Islam, seventh century.]

Admire with your heart, and flatter with your tongue.

To praise one who doesn't merit it is like putting a saddle of silk on an the back of an ass.
– KURDISH

F

It's the stomach that carries the two feet.
– TURKISH

The less food in the stomach, the more light in the heart.
– PERSIAN

Only the thistle can satisfy the camel.

Excess food makes one ill; excess wealth corrupts.

The stomach is the home of illness; keep your supper for your breakfast and you will be endowed with health.
– HADITH

FOOL

'I am coming in a carriage,' said the goose when carried away by the fox.

She is more fool than wise whose knowledge is more than her wisdom.

Explain to the crazy and they understand, yet fools won't change their minds.

You're a loser if you argue with a fool.

His head is big and empty like a dried pumpkin.

A light head makes the feet weary.

The astrologer spoke and fools listened.

Rather take from the fool than give to the wise.
[ALSO: Don't give a thing to the fool, lest she thinks of it as her own.]

To buy the manger, Bahlool sold the mule.

Flattery is the servitude of the low,
And the bosom friend of the prince;
Impostors go to it with soft soap
Giving him a wash with a crafty rinse.
– Lilminber

FOOD

Eat when hungry and cease while (still) hungry.
– HADITH

Don't make your stomachs a graveyard of beasts.
– HADITH

Wear what covers and eat what sustains.

A person's bread is a debt.
[Which they should repay to society.]

Those who live near water need not die of hunger.

F

The double fool

The miller once saw Bahlool taking flour from others' sacks and putting it into his own. 'Why are you doing that, Bahlool?' asked the miller. 'Because I'm a fool,' said Bahlool. 'But a fool would take from his own sack and fill others'!' said the miller. 'O, that would be a double fool!' responded Bahlool.

The first grade of folly is to hold oneself wise, the next is to profess it, and the worst is to refrain from asking for counsel and act on one's own.

FORCE

The wall asked the wedge: 'Why do you split me?'
'Ask the hammer on my head,' responded the wedge.

When force is the master, reason's house is the first to be demolished.

FORGETFULNESS

Forgetfulness is the bane of knowledge.

When a man rides his horse, he forgets about his God, and when he dismounts he forgets about the horse.
– PERSIAN

Forgetfulness is the cure of grievous memories.

FORGIVENESS

Forgiveness is perfect when the offense is forgotten.

They who forgive, God will forgive them.

Forgiveness from the heart is better than a box of gold.

My neighbors like me because I am rich, my friends like me because I am generous, and my husband likes me because I am forgiving.

If not for God's forgiveness, Paradise would remain empty.

'I forgive, but...' is not forgiveness.

Some ask forgiveness from those above them, but are too mean to give it to those below them.

Forgiveness is the virtue of victory.
– PERSIAN

Forgive your enemy and make them weaker.

49

F

The dog and the gazelle
A dog chased after a gazelle. 'You won't catch up with me,' said the gazelle. The dog asked why. 'Because you run for your master, and I run for my soul,' said the gazelle.

FRIENDSHIP

No road is too steep that leads to a friend.

A friend looks at your head; the foe looks at your feet.

No one is without an enemy, but no one should be without a friend.

Your friends are three: your friend, the friend of your friend and the enemy of your enemy. Your enemies are three: your enemy, the enemy of your friend and the friend of your enemy.

First befriend the dog.
– MALTESE

Do not forgive yourself for being weak, neither others for forgiving your weakness.
– Lilminber

They ask you what to give, say: 'Give forgiveness.'
– THE QUR'AN

FREEDOM

A free dog is stronger than a caged lion.

In a free land, the chief is called to account if he errs.
– PERSIAN

I asked freedom: 'Where are your children?' 'One passed away, one was made mad, one was hanged and one is not yet born,' she responded.
– KAHLIL GIBRAN (1883 - 1931), Lebanese mystical writer, poet and artist

F

Who would have friends, a foe's hate
must sustain,
Linked are snakes, gold; thorns, flowers;
joy and pain.
– SHEIKH SADI, thirteenth century Persian Sufi
poet

How many friends I had when my vines
yielded honey; how few they are now the
vines are dry!

A useless friend is like a harmless enemy.

A wise enemy is better than a foolish friend.

Beware of your enemy once and of your
friend twice.

Don't make friends with poets: they will
praise you for reward and censure you for
nothing.
[An old saying: such was the occupation of some poets
in ancient times.]

There are bones of a thousand friends in a
wolf's den.

Don't tell a friend a thing that you'd conceal
from an enemy.

Don't trust a new friend nor an old enemy.

You're my friend, not my purse's.

Don't rinse the cup of friendship with vinegar.

Benefit your friend with something that won't do you harm.

Inflict not on an enemy every injury
                in your power,
For he may some day change into
            a friend, like a brother.
– SHEIKH SADI, thirteenth century Persian Sufi poet

Sustain hunger for a year to entertain your friend for an hour.

Excuse your friend's faults in seventy ways.

How seldom you visit your friend, the fonder she will grow of you.

If you want to keep a friend don't take from her nor give to her.

If your friend is honey, don't lick him all up.

Reproach a friend lest you lose him.
[OR: Open reproach is better than hidden grudge.]

A new friend can't take the place of an old one.

One should travel a mile to visit a sick person, two miles to reconcile two people, and three miles to meet a friend.

Friends are counted at parting, not at meeting.

A narrow place is sufficient for a thousand friends; the whole world is not large enough for two enemies.

A friend is a mirror of his friend.

Two things are at their best when old: wine and friends.

F

In Heaven there is one God, and on Earth there is one friend.

An old friend is like a ready, saddled horse.

You may once need to wield your sword and then you need to lean upon a friend.

I go with her like water flowing downwards.

Here comes the sweetheart, there goes the friend.

A Bedouin was asked: 'Whom do you like more: a brother or a friend?'
'I won't like him if my brother is not my friend,' he said.

Life without a friend is pilaf without salt.
– UZBEK

A wise man was asked: 'Who is the one who travels farthest?'
'The one who is looking for a good friend,' came the answer.

Go to your friend when you are hungry, and pass no enemy whilst you are naked.

Live in a new house and stay with an old friend.

FUNERAL

Weddings take shouts, funerals take souls.

Bahlool was once asked whether it was more appropriate to walk behind or in front of the coffin at a funeral. 'Don't be inside the coffin and walk wherever you like,' he replied.

FUTURE

Squeeze the past like a sponge, smell the present like a rose and send a kiss to the future.

Past events foretell future ones.

Don't look too far ahead, lest you trip up.

There was the Door to which I found no key,
There was the Veil through which I might
                                    not see.
– OMAR KHAYYAM (1048 - 1131), Persian mathematician, astronomer and poet

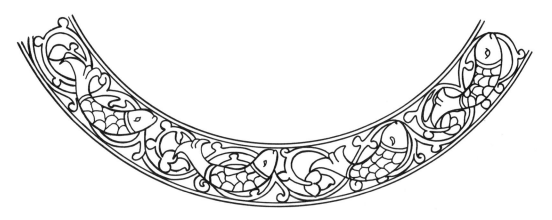

G

Some give not from generosity; others withhold not from miserliness.

'For collecting firewood she is grown-up and good, but for marriage she is too young yet!' protested the suitor's family when their son's suit was put off. 'Will gold get rusty, or will moisture harm wool?' came the answer.
– MOROCCAN

To examine an elephant, look at its tail; to observe a girl look at her mother.
– SUDANESE

GIVING

Sister gives out of love, stranger gives for gratitude.

We gave of what we were given.
[We did no special favor.]

All feed at his pasture.
[He is prosperous and open-handed.]

Feed the mouth to make the eye shy.

Generosity casts a long shadow.

Given a rope, you will be bound with it.
– PERSIAN

No one should give of what they haven't got.

It takes love to give, and to take with love is also giving.
– Lilminber

GIRL

Flowers break rocks.

She whose suitors are many is doomed to celibacy.
['Were she good enough, one of them would have married her.']

No one but her mother smelled under her armpit.
[Said of a virgin.]

G

A child gives of what it no longer needs.

A thing you use up will get rotten, a thing you give becomes a rose.

A present carried on an ass is to be repaid on a camel.

A small present comes from the heart, a big one from the pocket.
– TURKISH

Two madnesses are amongst virtues that make people great: courage and generosity.

You truly give when you give of yourself.
– KAHLIL GIBRAN (1883 – 1931), Lebanese mystical writer, poet and artist

They that give to be seen will relieve no one in the dark.

Good manners, restraint of anger and chastity of the eye are also giving.
– HADITH

Prayers carry us near the door of Paradise, and giving procures us admission.
– HADITH

God loves those who give.
– THE QUR'AN

GOD

In praise
'Allahu Akbar!'
['God is greater!' ('than your idols!') – first addressed by the Prophet to Arab idolaters, this remains an Islamic motto.]

'Allahu A'alam!'
['God knows better!' – said when one is not quite sure of an allegation or hearsay.]

Knowledge is manifold, God is one.

If God bestows you with luck, you won't need a thing more.

God's earth is boundless, and His creatures are free.

G

If you search for God, you will find Him.
[According to scholars, to 'find' God is to fulfill His commandments in the first place.]

No leaf of a tree moves but God
wills it.

He is the One who lets bad come out of good
and good out of bad.
– THE QUR'AN

God is the mother whom we forget with the first boon and remember with the first tear.

God dwells between a person and their heart.
God will reprove the seen and those who see.
[The person who sees a sin yet stays silent.]

If God shuts one door, He will open another.

For every harvest God sends a buyer with a measure.

It is He who creates us in an appealing form, and it is we who boast of it.

It is He who sways the cradle and He who grows the field.

Our sins go up to Him and His boons come down to us.

God fills men's stomachs without asking who their fathers are.
– TURKISH

G

Cocks crow, but it is God who breaks the dawn.

God asks for naught more than you can bear.
– THE QUR'AN

God's punishment
God does not throw stones.
[To punish the sinful, because He has other ways to chasten them.]

God delays but He never forgets.
[OR: God waits forty years. ALSO: God has a large belly.]

God sees what you will do,
In your Day He'll show it to you.

God's stick beats silently.

God does not raise a people or fell them but with what they do.

God's presence and deeds
God is closer to you than your jugular vein.

It is God who feels the pulse and God who gives the prescription.

God does not test us only with need, but also with abundance.

No one goes to God without His call.

God has sent a Prophet to every nation in their own tongue.

God will help those who rise early in the morning.

God gives sleep to the bad so that the good may be at rest.
– SHEIKH SADI, thirteenth century Persian Sufi poet

'Insha'alla' – God willing
[All will be fine!]

God has not sent rain to spread mud onto earth.

God has also given nuts to those who have no teeth.

God helps those who help themselves.

Our perceptions
No one has seen God with their own eyes.
To mention God's mercy is to ask for it.

They who search for God must put on a pair of wooden legs.
– PERSIAN
[So that they do not tire.]

G

Choose between dates and God!
[Dates symbolize here the mundane fortunes of the 'sweet' life.]

God says and I say!
[Said ironically to someone who disputes an acknowledged fact or axiom.]

Call on God but row away from the rocks.
– PERSIAN

God's language is silence, deeds without words, yet He likes us to utter them in defense of the wronged or to render a warning to our fellows.
– Overheard from a preacher

GOODNESS

Good words without deeds are like a fancy bowl without broth.
Don't do good, lest you receive evil.
[In contrast: We are bound by good turns.]

There is no good deed but some evil is linked to it.
[OR: Thorns yield roses and roses yield thorns.]

If you are able, that is what God wills for you; if you are able and good, that is what makes Him glad about you.
– HADITH

Throw good behind you, and you will find it ahead of you.

The farther good travels, the more it multiplies.

Hasten to do a good thing, for you are not always able to do it.

Evil will pass even if it lingers, good will stay even if it passed by.

Hide the good you do, like the Nile concealing its sources.

A handful of blessing is better than a hill of riches.

To defer doing good is bad, to defer bad is good.

To the pure, all things are pure.

Don't be clever, son, just be good.

Let it be that you be a nation that calls for good and forbids evil.
– THE QUR'AN

GOSSIP

Gossip, unlike river water, flows both ways.

He picked up gossip and spread it out.

Put me under people's feet, rather than on their tongues.

Gossip quarrels and tells the truth.

No spittle under a stone will remain covered.

An ill word spreads; a nice one stays at home.

Gossip is the talk of hell.
[It's a sin that deserves hellfire.]

Gossip is the effort of the weak.

Gossip is the conversation of fools.

She who conveys gossip to you will convey gossip about you too.

Would any of you like to eat his brother's flesh alive?
– THE QUR'AN

GRATITUDE

I must have been good to the one who remembered me (even) with a bone.

Thank her who did you a favor, and favor her who thanks you.

No burden is heavier than gratitude.
– TURKISH

Gratitude shows itself in three ways: in the heart, on the tongue and by the hand (ie by returning a favor in deed).

'To whom do you carry this glass of water?'
'To the one who once carried it full to me.'
[Water is of great value in the desert.]

When it drinks, even a hen raises its head up to heaven.

Even the dog knows the hand that feeds it.

Remember the old favor done to you, and forget about the new favor you do.

G

If you are thankful, I will grant you more.
– THE QUR'AN
[Scholars comment that thanksgiving in this context applies to good deeds rather than good words alone.]

GRAY HAIR

Gray hair is welcome, before shameful deeds.

You can't walk on your head but when it becomes gray.
– PERSIAN

Gray hair is a torch of wisdom.

'Is my hair white or black?'
'You'll see it when it falls down,' answered the barber.

Death sends its message in gray hair.

Gray hair causes no shame, but shame causes gray hair.

Fallen leaves don't shame a good tree.

An old man was asked about the state of the world. 'My hair has not turned white in a flour-mill,' he said.

Youth in old age is more pleasant than old age in youth.

When a lion gets old, foxes start to laugh at him.

No rage, no old age.

If the youth knew, or the old could.
– PERSIAN
[Then the face of the world would change.]

Time did not give me my gray hair
for nothing:
I paid cash for it with the youth of my life.
But if you ask me what I've got out of it,
Torn by sorrow and blest by joy, in
endless strife.
– SHEIKH SADI, thirteenth century Persian Sufi poet who lived to a ripe old age.

GREED

Greed is a constant slavery.

Greed is the poverty of the present.

A free person is a slave when greedy, and a slave is free when contented.

Men collapse under the flash of greed.

G

She neither retained her husband nor married Abu Ali!

Vinegar free of charge is sweet honey to the greedy mouth.
[ALSO: 'Free arrack (strong liquor)? Kadi will drink!' Alcohol is prohibited in Islam; a kadi is a judge.)

The greedy mouth can be filled up but by the earth of the grave.

If you are covetous you are a prisoner, if you are greedy you will never be filled.

He gives little and takes much.
Rather the cold of despair than the heat of greed.

The greedy one's beard is up the arse of the one who is broke.

Going to get horns, the sheep lost its ears.

He wants the sparrow and its thread.
[Of an aggressively greedy person. The saying uses the metaphor of a possessive child playing with a tethered little bird.]

He swallowed a camel and wondered what it was!
[Of a glutton.]

We coveted their sheep; they stole our camels.

Had the greedy person a valley of gold, they would still look for another.

Don't take your hand out of his mouth!
[If still you need something to be done by him.]

Sands brought by wind will be blown by the storm.

The greedy one was once told to take half the world and keep quiet. 'What about the other half?' he asked.

Greed is a vehicle pushed by fear of need and pulled by striving to power, but it often breaks down midway.
– Lilminber

A single loaf the stomach will supply;
But not earth's richest gifts the greedy eye.
– SHEIKH SADI, thirteenth century Persian Sufi poet

If you expel avarice from your heart, the fetter will be loosened from your feet.
– SHEIKH SADI

GROWTH

Don't underestimate the few that will multiply, nor the little thing that will grow.
– IMAM ALI, seventh century, the fourth Khalif of Islam

A cow's ears grow first, but its horns grow longer.
– TURKISH

A hair and a hair will become a beard.

The small won't become big until the big become small.
[Of children and their parents who bring them up.]

There is a tree under every stone (in the field).

What belongs to God will grow.

H

If cats and rats agree, the town will be brought to ruin.

Habit is the guide of the narrow-minded.

He who grew up on a dunghill keeps longing for it.

The tailor was invited to come out for a picnic: he fixed the needle into his fez and came along.
  – LEVANTINE

We weave the thin threads of our lives into the unbreakable ropes of habit.
  – PERSIAN

HAND-IN-GLOVE

Hold for me, I'll cut for you.
[When two scoundrels work hand-in-glove.]

When the ruler is a tyrant, the judge is his hangman.

HABIT

Habit is contentment.

Even worship is a habit.

Only the shroud can change a habit.

He who is used to your bread and soup will rinse his mouth when he sees you from afar.

She who changes her ways loses her happiness.

The waves made friends with the wind at the expense of the ship.

You, hush... me, hush!
[Let us share it between us!]

The onlooker is an accomplice.
[Said of those who passively witness a misdeed without helping.]

H

People are three: the one who searches for happiness but won't find it, the one who can be happy but is not, and the happy one who is not aware of it.

Bahlool's happiness
A story goes that Bahlool once passed by a graveyard in a foreign land and noticed on the tombs that the dead had lived very short lives. He was curious, and was told that the number of years inscribed on the gravestones were only the happy periods of their lives. Bahlool then thought for a moment and said: 'Please write on mine: Bahlool came out of his mother and went right into the grave.'

They were a gang of two: the thief and the fortune-teller.
– IRAQI
[People in ancient Baghdad used to go to fortune-tellers for help in finding thieves.]

HAPPINESS

Your sense of happiness will be enhanced if you transfer it to others.
– KAHLIL GIBRAN (1883-1931), Lebanese mystical writer, poet and artist

It is wise to enjoy yourself, but it is a virtue to create enjoyment.
– SHEIKH SADI, thirteenth century Persian Sufi poet

The gown of happiness is soft and smooth.

Joy has almost reached the threshold.

Common grief is joy.
– TUNISIAN

HARVEST

A good harvest is sown by good hands.

If you count little birds, you won't sow the seeds.

If you plant roses in the mean one's soil, you'll reap but thorns.
– KURDISH

HASTE

Haste is of the devil.
– HADITH

No sooner had he kissed her than it kicked!
[She conceived and the embryo began to kick. Used satirically for people in a hurry.]

At the sound of the drum, O my feet, be light!

If you want to do it quickly, do it slowly.

H

The person in a hurry does it badly twice.

Seeing her folk unrolling their tents, she said, 'Find me a husband first!'

Error is the companion of the one in a hurry.

A poor person in a hurry is on their way to serving a rich one.

Haste comes from the devil save on three occasions: to bury the dead, entertain a guest and marry a woman.
– HADITH

HATRED

Love comes down from heaven; hatred has no good place to come from.
– HADITH

If you hate leave a place for love, but if you love leave no place for hatred.

Hate while you fear.
– PERSIAN

Hate eats up the hater's heart and gladdens her foe's.

Love and cover; hate and uncover (faults, etc).

I was sick of you, and you visit me now in my sickness?!

The house of hate is built with bricks of harm.

If you dislike someone don't deny them their rights.

HAZARDS

No camel knows which stone will cause it to stumble.

May God save us from fire, drowning and dying at the side of the road.

People go about their business, devils go about people's hazards.

He drank the sea and was choked by the stream.

HEALING

Here is your medicine, but with God lies your recovery.

Finding the cure

The story goes that a traveler arrived in a town on the back of his donkey, which had injuries due to the length of the journey. He looked in vain for something that would treat it quickly. Then he passed by a man and asked his advice.

'I can tell you how to heal your donkey, traveler; but I need my fee in advance,' said the man. Once he had received his due fee, the man raised his face to the traveler and told him: 'Leave the donkey alone, and it will heal on its own!'

[The moral is that it takes a break from work, relaxation and rest to heal a malady – an obvious thing which escapes the minds of some of the sick and some healers as well.]

HEALTH

If you have health you have hope, and if you have hope you have everything.
– PERSIAN

Much argument causes liver complaints.
– PERSIAN

Health and extravagance won't stay together. Life comes from heaven, health comes from contented stomachs.

No one is a good doctor who has never been ill.

The bitterness of medicine is the sweetness of recovery.

To be in good health is a constant feast.

Bid 'Good day' to the bean-dealer, not to the druggist.

My health is better than my wealth, my ankles are better than my ankle-rings, and my ears are better than my earrings.
– IRAQI

The stomach is the home of illness.
– HADITH

Cheerfulness is a sign of health.

HEAVEN

Heav'n is but the Vision of fulfill'd desire;
And Hell, the shadow from a soul on fire.
– OMAR KHAYYAM (1048 – 1131), Persian mathematician, astronomer and poet

In heaven ambition cannot dwell:
No bargain to strike, nothing to sell.
– Lilminber

HELP

If a dog helps you cross the river don't ask if it has mange.

If you want to fall into the well, Providence

H

won't come to your aid.
– PERSIAN

They who cannot harm cannot afford help either.

Let us first reach her before we can give her a hand.

When your coach has turned over, people come to show you the way.

Preach help to no one before you extend your hand to them.
– PERSIAN

HELPLESSNESS

Only the dead are helpless.
– KURDISH

HEREDITY

Young or old, the hawk has a beak.

The white dogs and the black dogs are all sons of bitches.

The scorpion is the cousin of the serpent.
[Both are deadly.]

The hedgehog put its hand on its children and was glad they were all prickly.

The duck's chick is a floater.
[OR: The man who descended from dogs would bark.]

Only a mule disowns its father.
[When asked who its father was, the mule said: 'My uncle is the horse.']

Will a snake beget but a snake?

Only a crow looks like its father.

HIDING

One cannot hide a spear under the armpit.

He who can steal a minaret can hide it too.

She rode a camel and sought a hiding-place behind the sheep.

HOME

If you are at home take your time.

You provide from without, and I manage from within, and so we build our home together.
[Sumerian wife, to her husband.]

Every person is a child at home.

H

There is a road for a man to ride, and a home for him to live in.

A house is where one lives, and a home is where one takes refuge.

Hand with hand we build a home, heart with heart we keep it.

In every home there is a sewer.
[To hide its secrets, or perhaps to 'drain' its wealth, or both.]

It was a patient woman who built her own home.

Rather a hut where my soul flutters than a castle where I am bound to walls.
[In an old poem, a Bedouin woman to her princely husband.]

None should stay the night outside but the lock on the door.
– TUNISIAN

HOMELAND

Love of one's homeland is a sign of faith.
– HADITH

Poverty in one's homeland is estrangement, wealth in exile is a homeland.

They are no longer in their homeland, but their homeland is still in them.

HONESTY

Walk right with the lame and talk straight with the crooked.

An honest person can but tear their garments.
[In desperation at the crooked ways of the world.]

Sincerity is the pearl that forms inside the shell of the heart.
– SUFI

Honesty makes its own way whilst it goes; dishonesty has to search out narrow lanes to zigzag through.
– Lilminber

HONOR

Defend your household before your gold, and your honor before your land.

The fault is in the pocket that the honor is pierced.

H

A head without pride is to be cut off.

Credibility is gain, ill name is loss.

HOPE

Bahlool threw up his turban and said: 'Between its going up and coming down there will be a thousand hopes.'

He was hanging by ropes of wind.

Amidst despair there is hope; behold, the black night comes to an end at the white dawn.
– SHEIKH SADI, thirteenth century Persian Sufi poet

Hope is a comrade: if it doesn't bring you up to your journey's end, it will yet entertain you on the road.
– SHEIKH SADI

If one door shuts, another will open.

HOSPITALITY

A noble person is apt to open their door.

The guest of a hospitable person will learn hospitality.

The first guest is the host of the second.
– IRAQI

A guest is the owner of the house for three days.

This is 'your' house, the mosque will yet be warmer for you!
[An inhospitable host.]

HOUSE

They laid brick over brick and so they built a house.
– SUMERIAN

With hand and hand, a man's house is built; with stomach and stomach, it is pulled down.
– SUMERIAN

A house is not to look at but to live in.
– PERSIAN

Rather a grave over a grave than a house over house.

If you see someone sitting in the street, you may guess that they are more comfortable there than in their own house.

Two in a grave are more comfortable than two in a house.
[Of incompatible people living together.]

A house full of people is better than a house full of gold.

H

Were it not for the deceased, the living could not dwell in their houses.

Take for thieves all who enter your house, and your house will be safe.

A house should be the first thing to buy and the last to sell.

Seek a comrade before the road, and a neighbor before the house.
[BUT: We didn't sell the house, but the neighbor.]

HUMILITY

Call someone your master and he will sell you in the slave market.

If you build your wall low many will jump over it.

She who makes herself a bone will be eaten by dogs.

Don't be a vineyard at the side of the road.

One could load the camel as it agreed to kneel.

The least light falls on the legs of the lamp.
– TURKISH

The head which is bowed will escape the swordsman's eyes.

The firmest stone in the building is down in the foundation.

Humility in someone of high position lifts them still higher.

Humility is a net to ensnare the lofty.
– PERSIAN

Modesty is the sweet songbird, which no open door can tempt to fly away.
– SHEIKH SADI, thirteenth century Persian Sufi poet

To be humble is fine, but take care not to be humiliated.

He who has no faith has no humility.
– HADITH

HUNGER

An empty stomach has no ears.

The thirsty one breaks the water jar.

When a snake is hungry, it bites its own abdomen.

Hunger begets impiety.
[OR: No hungry person ever worshipped God.]

Hunger is housed in the body, satisfaction is housed in the soul.

A hungry one would wound the sword.

One died of an empty stomach, another of a full one.

Hunger is the best condiment.

To be content with hope is to die of hunger.

I wonder how a man, finding nothing to eat at home, may not set out wielding his sword on people around him.
– ABU THAR AL-GHIFARI, one of the Prophet's companions

HUNTING

An eagle doesn't chase flies.

A fisher needs troubled waters.
– TURKISH

A hunter's intentions are in his quiver.

Hunting for pleasure is savagery in leisure.
– Lilminber

The hunter and the hunted will both go to their God.

Those who hunt not for sustenance should not scare the beasts.
– HADITH

HUSBAND

Better a neat bed than a messy husband.

Still at the graveyard, he is looking for a beauty.
[Of a recent widower.]

The new husband is a new dress, the second husband is a patch.

For the first seven years, he was my rose; for the second seven years, he did my need; for the third seven years, he looked for my fortune; and for the fourth seven years, he was on his own and I was on mine.
– LEVANTINE

My husband tells me lies and I tell them to my neighbors.

HYPOCRISY

A fox sees with its eyes and covers with its tail.

Many a man kisses the hand he wishes to cut off.

O, my dead slave! Now I will set you free!

Face-to-face she is a mirror, behind the back she is a thorn.

The devil is the teacher of hypocrisy who, once his pupils are 'good at it', starts to ridicule them.

A fox imprisoned in the hen-house, said he feared the hens would peck him dead.

Who would ever dare say the mouth of the lion stinks?
[The lion here implies a tyrant rather than someone brave.]

A tiger is savage when it attacks a man, but a man is a hunter when he shoots a tiger.

To curse the devil in public while one is his friend in secret.

'Don't bother, don't bother!' he protested whilst putting it under his turban.
[Of a 'present' to the kadi or judge.]

Like water, some take the color of every vessel they are poured in.

After his death, his bottom started to exude honey.
[Implying that all of a sudden the deceased one had become 'dear and sweet' to his inheritors.]

She echoed words like the vault of a bathhouse.
[Loud and empty.]

He saw the camel, and he didn't see the camel.

'Mourning you, Bu Touma, makes me drink much, too much!'
– LEVANTINE
[The exclamation of a woman who made a mourning feast for the husband she had disliked alive. She ate heartily for the joy of the occasion, and drank ostensibly to show sorrow at his passing.]

I

The devil tempts all, the idler tempts all devils.

IDLENESS

An idler on top of a camel will soon learn to travel.

Water left in the jar will soon go bad.

For the idle are sinners too.

He castrates flies, didn't you know?

No arm to work with, no face to beg with. The idler's back is salty.
[No work and no bathing!]

If an egg had two handles, it would take two idlers to carry it.

The sleeping donkey has lost its fodder.

He cuts streets and tailors quarters.

Lazybones and his wife

An old Persian story goes that a listless man living in a remote place out in the desert thought that poverty was glory in the sight of God. But he had a wife who told him that God asked men to go and find themselves some ways and means for earning their livelihood. At long last she managed to convince him, and so he asked her what to do next. She told him to go and carry a sack of water and stand by the side of the road, for a start. It happened on that day that a prince had gone astray in the middle of the desert and met with this poor man who immediately quenched his thirst. The prince thanked him for saving his life and filled his sack with coins that made him rich. In this manner this poor man was shown that to rise and act was pleasing to God.

IGNORANCE

The empty sack can't stand upright.
– TURKISH

The ignorant person is her own enemy, how could she be your friend?

I

The ignorance that I master, rather than the knowledge that masters me.

He that knows not and knows not that he knows not – shun him.

If you argue with the ignorant, you'll be beaten.

Malice is the chosen weapon of the ignorant. – UZBEK

ILLNESS

Scabies is not shameful; it's shameful not to seek a cure.

Smoke that blinds rather than cold that makes sick.

Cold and poverty are the source of all illness. – IMAM ALI, seventh century, the fourth Khalif of Islam

Illness is the purification of the body; repentance is the purification of the soul. – SHEIKH SADI, thirteenth century Persian Sufi poet

IMITATION

One gazelle came and drank; the whole herd followed suit.

Imitation is blind praise.

Imitations can excel the original, yet the merit belongs to the latter.

IMPERFECTIONS

There is no beauty without a flaw.

Faults are overlooked by the loving eye, assets are coveted by the envious one.

To live with imperfections is a virtue of the wise. – PERSIAN

INCLINATION

It is written on the sparrow's wings: 'I can't help flying to those I love to see.'
[OR: One's feet take one where one's heart wants to go.]

Other people, other inclinations.

Your heart shows the direction, and the mind shows the way. – Lilminber

INDIFFERENCE

The one who lost his aunt's donkey would sing if he found it and sing if he didn't.

A donkey that I got off – let it be ridden by 'monkeys'.

INFAMY

All beasts are savage, but the wolf is infamous.
[OR: All birds peck, the infamy is of the sparrow.]

(He is) a bell tied to the tail of a mule.
– LEVANTINE
[He is a scandalmonger.]

Let an eye rather than a name go bad.
– PERSIAN

Disrepute is a shabby gown evoking frowns round the town.

INGRATITUDE

We let her in, she let us out.

He who gives no thanks to people will give no thanks to God.

When harm is added to ingratitude, the injury is complete.
– PERSIAN

Don't throw stones into the well from which you drink.

I gave the lame person a ride, but she put her hand into my sack from behind.

One hand into the (host's) plate, another into the (host's) eyes.

Beware of those to whom you have done a good turn.

Don't spit into the plate where you have eaten.
[OR: He ate the broth and broke the dish.]

The heart of the ungrateful person is like desert sand: it swallows water but it doesn't grow plants.

Ingratitude is the twin of vanity.

A thankful dog is better than an ungrateful person.

 **I**

He raised the ax on the tree, and it said to him: 'Strike – the handle comes from me, anyway.'

God's blessing comes down to us, and our sins go up to Him.

Every day I taught him how to shoot:
As his arm strengthened he aimed at me;
How often I showed him how to write verses:
Once he mastered them he censured me.

INJURY

The stricken one may forget, but not the striker.

I am the servant of the one who favors me and the master of the one who slanders me.
– TURKISH

She who is contemptuous of an injury won't return it in kind.

An injury by relatives causes more pain than iron and steel.

The whole world united against you can't harm you as much as you can yourself.

To repeat an apology is to recall the offense.

INNOCENCE

The innocent one was beaten so that the culprit would confess.

If your 'account' is clean, fear no king or queen.

Innocence can defend itself.

When the dry hay burnt, the green hay burnt too.

INTENTION

Deeds are judged by intentions.

I

It started as a jest and ended as a tragedy.

Do you want to kill the watchman, or (just) eat the grapes?

They are fools who can't read the heart before the tongue speaks.
– TURKISH

Those used to evil ways readily suspect others' intentions.

Hell is full of good intentions.
– PERSIAN

INTIMACY

Intimacy casts out formality.

Affectionate to our friends and intimate with the beloved.

INTRIGUE

The thief was told to 'carry on', and the household to be on their guard.

A hay serpent bites and hides its head.

An enemy inside the house can do more harm than a thousand outside.

If you dig a pit for your neighbor, dig it to your size.

Why should you kill him with poison if you could with honey?

If I invite you to enter my house don't ask me to enter the grave.

Launch sedition from your house and it will come back to you.

INTRUSION

A guest without invitation is to sit without salutation.

Onwards, my friends, onwards without fear,
And spare no party of a prince or emir!
– A gatecrasher to his companions in ancient Baghdad

J

The horse rider was the culprit, the kadi (judge) ruled to hang the muleteer.

JEALOUSY

When a palm-tree looks at her sister, both bear fruit.

The jealous one is not fit to lead.

JESTING

Jest with an ass, and it will swat you in the face with its tail.

Don't jest with a child unless you are its father; don't tease a woman unless you are her man.

Laugh with people and weep alone.

JUDGE (Kadi)

He who goes alone to the kadi will return with satisfaction.

A present gouges the eye of the kadi.
[OR: The touchstone proves the gold and the gold proves the kadi.]

When the ruler is a tyrant, the kadi becomes his hangman.

Were people fair, the kadi would stay in poverty.
[OR: Let us pray the kadi's fortune is halal! (ie legally earned)]

For every kadi in paradise, two burn in hellfire.

All men's teeth are blunted by sour things except the kadi's, whose edge is taken off by 'sweets'.
– SHEIKH SADI, thirteenth century Persian Sufi poet

Woe to those whose judges are their culprits.

The children's judge hung herself.
[She was not able to judge between them.]

Bahlool's encounters with the kadi

The story goes that a man hit Bahlool on his nape in public by way of scorning him. Bahlool caught the rogue by his collar and took him to the kadi. However, the man happened to be one of the kadi's friends. The kadi declared that Bahlool may either hit the man on the back of his neck in return or take fifty dinars in damages. Bahlool, being poor, preferred to take the money. The kadi then asked the culprit whether he had the money on him already. He then got the message and asked for permission to leave the court to fetch the fine. Bahlool waited and waited in vain. He finally came up to the kadi, gave him a hard hit on the back of his neck and said to him: 'When your friend comes back with the money, take it from him in damages, your Honor.'

* * *

Another story goes that a police agent fetched two men to the court and presented his case saying that he had found some garbage lying between their house-doors and asked them to remove it, but each of them said it was the responsibility of the other. Bahlool happened to be present in the court for business of his own. The kadi, jealous of Bahlool's high standing in the eyes of the people, thought to put him in a difficult situation by referring the case to him for judgment.

Bahlool thought for a moment and accepted. Then he proceeded to ask the constable: 'Was the garbage nearer to the door of this or that man?' The constable replied that it was found bang in the middle. Bahlool then pondered for a little while and said to the kadi: 'Since the garbage was found in the public street, it is the duty of the kadi to remove it, as it is you who are the one in charge of the welfare of the city, your Honor.'

JUDGMENT

The strongest of people will fall to fate if they have no judgment.
– SUMERIAN

If all men did not make hasty judgments, all would end up in Paradise.
– HADITH

A wise person can judge things better, a shrewd person can judge others better.

JUSTICE

The rope of justice is long.

It is not justice to speed up justice.

You who heard of my indictment, won't you hear of my plight?

The Sultan's justice is better than the prosperity of the land.

The hand of a just man is a good scale.

Were both rivals fair, they would need no judge for justice.

Justice is good, but no one wants it in their own house.

J

Justice is often a stick in the hands of the unjust.

One hour in the execution of justice is worth seventy years of worship.
– HADITH

Bahlool's justice
Bahlool was one day riding his donkey with the saddlebag on his shoulder. People looked and laughed, wondering why he was doing that.

'That is quite just,' said Bahlool, 'as the donkey is carrying me I should carry the saddlebag for it.'

The wall of justice
One of Khalif Omar's viceroy's wrote to him asking permission to build a wall for his city. Omar replied: 'What is the use of walls? Fortify your city with justice and cleanse its ways of oppression!'

K

Kindness out of season destroys authority.
– PERSIAN

KINDNESS

Kind hearts don't grow old.

Learn kindness from the unkind.

With gentleness the fracture is repaired.

A kind word with forgiveness is better than giving followed by injury.
– THE QUR'AN

Bahlool & the KING

The King once asked Bahlool, 'Bahlool, if gold and justice were put before you, which one would you take?'

'I would take the gold,' said Bahlool.

'Why, Bahlool?' asked the King. 'As for me, I would certainly take justice, because justice is quite difficult to find.'

'Surely, everyone looks for what is missing from them, your Majesty,' responded Bahlool.

✳ ✳ ✳

The King and his chief minister went out hunting one day with Bahlool. As it was a very warm day, the two statesmen took off their garments and gave them to Bahlool to carry on his shoulder.

'Oh Bahlool, you are a strong man; the burden you are carrying is heavy enough for an ass!'

'No, your Majesty! On my shoulder there is a burden of two asses already,' retorted Bahlool quietly.

✳ ✳ ✳

Bahlool had a spell suffering from double vision. By way of ridicule, the King pointed at Bahlool's donkey and asked him to look at it.

'Bahlool, is it true that when you look at a thing it becomes two?' asked the King mockingly. 'Lo and behold, you are rich now. Look, you have two donkeys already!'

'You are right. Now I see you, just like my donkey, having four feet too, your Majesty.'

✳ ✳ ✳

As the King could no longer sustain his displeasure with Bahlool, he ordered him to be hanged. Bahlool's wife came to see him off at the gallows. The King, however, was amazed to notice a bulge in his loins and

cont'd

K

Knowledge is the best of treasures: it is light to carry around, not vulnerable to theft and useful in time of need.
– AL-RADHI, tenth century scholar

Whoever acquires knowledge but does not use it is one who plows but does not sow.
– PERSIAN

Alas! When I was able I didn't know, and when I know I am no longer able.
– SHEIKH SADI, thirteenth century Persian Sufi poet

Knowledge is the perennial spring of wealth – and of itself it is riches.
– SHEIKH SADI

asked him how that could happen to him at such a moment. 'Your mind, my wife's and that of "the thing in here" are of a kind, your Majesty,' said Bahlool.

KISS

A kiss without love burns the mustaches.

Kiss a woman's hand in love and a man's head in friendship.

How many a hand is kissed whilst wishing it cut off!

KNOWLEDGE

Doubt is the key of knowledge.
– SHEIKH SADI, thirteenth century Persian Sufi poet

All things but knowledge would diminish if used.
[Knowledge, however, grows.]

K

Knowledge is not culture, in the same way that building materials are not the mosque.
– TURKISH

Religion disperses, kingdoms fall apart, but works of knowledge remain for all ages.
– ULUG BEG (1393-1449), mathematician and astronomer; carved on his observatory in Samarkand

One does not become a scholar by licking the ink.

The black ink dispels the darkness of ignorance and lights up the lamp of the mind.
– IBN UL-MUQAFFA, ninth century writer

Knowledge is nearer to silence than to talk.

No one can take from knowledge more than one can understand.

A scholar's guess is nearer the truth than a fool's certitude.

A person's knowledge is used everyday.

We are born with our minds, not with knowledge.
– BEDOUIN

A learned person who doesn't act is like a cloud without rain.
– PERSIAN

Knowledge is the adornment of the mind, and the first stage to acquiring it is to cleanse the mind of the dust of arrogance first.

Learning is like healing: it comes step by step.

The more of knowledge the more of doubt.

It is better to know than not to know.

Take wisdom (even) from the side of the road.
– HADITH

The ink of men of knowledge is more sacred than the blood of martyrs.
– HADITH

For every gain you shall pay zaka (tax), and the zaka for gaining knowledge is to pass it on to your fellow people.
– HADITH

Let those who have knowledge be honored.
– HADITH

If you miss a meal, bless it; if you miss the news, go and search for it.

If one learns songs at an old age, one will only sing them in heaven.

Once he died a charm was hung on his chest.
[To ward off the evil eye.]

There is good in every delay.
[OR: Delay evil, and it will be good; delay good, and it will be evil.]

LAUGHTER

A mishap that made you cry, and another that made you laugh.

His face doesn't laugh, not even for a warm loaf of bread.

Laughter spoils the sale.

She laughed like a walnut cracked between two stones.

The camel laughed and laughed until its lip split open.

LATENESS

Your sun is high!
[You are late!]

Your cousin was taken whilst you were still tying the cord of your underpants.

She was slower than Noah's crow!
[Legend relates that Noah sent the crow to see if the flood had ebbed, but it lingered behind for far too long.]

The late one will bring you the latest news.

What is deferred is not abandoned.

LAW

Laws act after crime; prevention acts before it.

Law is the salt of the earth.

One law for the sultan and another for his people.

L

When the judge is not your friend, stay away from the courthouse.

Bad laws are the burden of good people, and bad people are the burden of good laws.
– Lilminber

LAWYERS

Poor are those who go to court, rich are their lawyers.

He who opens a case will open the floodgates.
– TURKISH

LAZINESS

Laziness is the key to the house of poverty.

The lazy one stood up: a whole town was pulled down.

A lazy person on a camel's back will learn to travel.

LEADERSHIP

Their leader is their servant.

Many a chieftain ruins the land.
[OR: A ship would sink if it had no captain, and it would sink if it had two.]

If you take a cock for your guide, you will end up sleeping in the hen house.

It is easier to lead a herd of a thousand camels than a company of two men.

There is no finer complement to leadership than clemency.

If the big one is absent, the small ones will fall to arguing..

LEARNING

What you learn young will stay for long.

He learnt himself and taught his mother too.
[The clever boy.]

Wanting to know how to walk, a sparrow learnt how to hop.
[One can't learn something against one's own character.]

I learnt silence from the talkative, tolerance from the intolerant, and kindness from the unkind. Yet, strangely enough, I am not grateful to these teachers.
– KAHLIL GIBRAN (1883 - 1931), Lebanese mystical writer, poet and artist

After gray hair, she went to learn in the fair!
[Grown-ups are bad learners.]

L

He who doesn't bear the pressure of learning today will have to sustain the burden of ignorance tomorrow.
– FIRDOUSI, twelfth century Persian author of the epic *Shahnama*

It takes ten pounds of common sense to carry a pound of learning.
– SHEIKH SADI, thirteenth century Persian Sufi poet

The more you learn, the sadder you become; but then the instructions of sorrow are the genuine learning.
– PERSIAN

Learn from the cradle to the grave.
– HADITH

When the schoolmaster gentle is and sweet,
The boys will play at leapfrog in the street.
– SHEIKH SADI

LEISURE

Leisure is the Devil's vocation.

Take a good hour to redeem a thousand bad ones.

One hour for your God, another for your soul.

LENDING

Give with your hand and run with your feet.
[In order to collect what you lent.]

Lending nurses displeasure.

Lending is the scissors of friendship.

Lend to me today, my heirs will surely pay.
– TUNISIAN

Light up with your hair, but don't ask your aunt for fire.

A borrowed garment won't fit.
[OR: You cannot ride a borrowed horse for long.]

The borrowed jar is haunted by the devil.

Don't lend a thing to a fool, lest she might think it is her own.

Don't borrow for pleasure, you'll regret it; nor for vanity for it'll end in shame.

You are rich when not in need; you are poor when you borrow (even) a reed.

He who does not want to lend a rope would say he wants to hang his grain on it.

LIFE

Life is an egg on the head of a horn.
– MALAYSIAN

L

Life is a handful of ice under the summer sun.
– PERSIAN

In the same way the sun has a shadow, a person's shadow is their work in life.
– AFGHAN

Life is pregnant with wonders.

Life is a dream, from which death wakes us.

The living dead and the dead living.

Nothing is eternal, but life stories have no end.

Your 'stars' are in the heavens, but your feet are on earth.

Whosoever does right, whether male or female, and is faithful, verily We quicken him with good life.
– THE QUR'AN

LIMITS

Don't stretch your steps too wide lest you split in two.

Stretch your feet up to the your bedcover.
[OR: Measure your appetite to your plate.]

Blest is the one who knows his limits and halts at them.
– HADITH

LOOKS

Look at your face in the mirror every morning. If it looks nice to you at that moment, you must have then done something good the previous day; otherwise go and cover it up with a nice deed first thing in the morning.
– IMAM ALI, seventh century, the fourth Khalif of Islam

'Your hair looks nice today!'
'The henna bush knows about that.'
[Henna is a small plant whose leaves are dried and ground into powder. It is widely used in the Arabic world to dye hair, hands and feet with an attractive red tint. In Morocco a guest is welcomed with a long session of henna decoration on their hands and feet.]

That which Abu Ali has got shows upon Abu Ali.

LOT (Kismet)

Everyone is contented with their mind, but no one with their lot.

The one-eyed weep and the two-eyed weep; the widower weeps and the one with two wives weeps; the one who has weeps and the one who has not weeps; the trader weeps and the one living from-hand-to-mouth weeps; kings weep and their servants weep. One can but wonder whom this world was supposed to make laugh.

L

Love comes down from heaven, hatred has no good place to come from.

In love and escape you don't need counsels.

The older the flame of love, the higher it rises.

Hearts are healed when rejoined in love.

A loving eye won't see a fault.

Love is proved in time of parting.

Love, perfume and camel riding can't be concealed.

Pay heed to the pitfall when you glance at your beloved at the corner of the road.

A dog was asked why it ate bones. 'That is my lot,' it replied.

Let the skinny goat be your lot rather than let the stout one go to the wolf.

One cooked the rooster, another had it for a meal.

And this was all the harvest that I reap'd:
I came like water, and like wind I go.
– OMAR KHAYYAM (1048 - 1131), Persian mathematician, astronomer and poet

LOVE

The heart isn't a table set for every passer-by.

Love is a sweet whose juice is delicious but whose shell is bitter.
– PERSIAN

Love doesn't ask for beauty, but beauty asks for love.
– Lilminber

How lovely to live for those whom you love.

Love is a passing traveler that cuts its journey short for the coolness of the place.
['Coolness' here implies 'comfort'. 'Heart-cooling' in an Arabic context means what is implied by 'heart-warming' in Western culture on account of the different climates.]

To resist a new temptation is to keep old love new.

Love ought to be like a camel's palanquin: well balanced on both sides.

If you can't enter through the door of love, enter through the gate of silver.

The vessel of love can't be filled up.

Nearness without love is a house without a ceiling.

The eye of love is blind.

Talk so that I can hear you, walk so that I can look at you!

If you are loved go and sleep in security.
[OR: If a serpent loved you, you might wear it round your neck.]

Up in heaven there is one God, and down on earth there is one beloved.

The needle takes one thread and the heart takes one sweetheart.

She loved him with the eye of her heart, and he loved her with the heart of his eye.

Once love is in, ethics are out.

He who travels won't mind the night, and he who is in love won't mind the rocky hills.
– TURKISH

Love is latent in the soul like fire in the flint stone.

Once the beloved has entered, kith and kin need not stay on.

Love and poverty – no sooner they meet than they part; their bed is deprivation and their cover is mistrust.

Love is fire, reason is smoke – if the fire comes in the smoke will go out.

Love is the madness that leads us back to our reason.
– Lilminber

I loved him but he didn't love me; he tired my heart and he tired me.

The one in love thinks people are blind, but they think she's mad.

Hearts complement hearts.

Lust is the daughter of love but she strays.

Lust is the shell, not the kernel, of love.

If I win in the duel of love you're mine, if you win I'm yours.
– PERSIAN

He with whom a woman falls in love, the sun becomes his cousin.

Don't take love without giving it.

Who is in love with himself will be hated by others.

She who lived in love would die without a sin.

L

Ah Love! could you and I with Fate conspire
To grasp this sorry scheme of things entire;
Would not we shatter it to bits – and then
Remold it nearer to the Heart's desire.
– OMAR KHAYYAM (1048 - 1131), Persian
mathematician, astronomer and poet

Before today I used to disown my friend,
If his creed was not akin to mine;
But my heart now has become a pasture
For gazelles, and a monastery for monks –
A temple for idols and a Kaaba for a pilgrim,
A sheet of the Bible and a page in the Qur'an.
I do now have faith in Love – and with it
I journey wherever its caravan heads,
For love now is my faith and conviction.
– IBN UL-ARABI (1165-1240), Sufi mystic

No matter how many the obstacles on the
way to (the beloved) Leila's home, so long as
the first step is madness in love.
– HAFIZ, fourteenth century Persian poet

LOVER

Take a prince as a lover and pick up pearls
forever.

'Hey, you, whore! Here is a dirham, come on
with me to those hills!'
'Is that for your sweet tongue, for your
fortune or for the nearness of the place?'
retorted the prostitute.
[A dirham was a small silver coin, one-twentieth the
value of a dinar in Iraq.]

He came in vigilant and went out drowsy.

If she were in the mood, she would give it
(even) through a brick wall.

It was noise not love.

LUCK

Bad luck
You are put in water, the water becomes foul;
you are put in the garden, the fruits begin to
rot.
– SUMERIAN
[Of misfits]

If your luck becomes a stone, carry it with you.

When he started to trade in shrouds, people
stopped dying.

All your life, O raisin, a stick is stuck into your
bottom.
[Of someone who constantly has problems.]

The unlucky mouse sees the cheese, but not
the cat.

If your bad luck is asleep, don't wake it up.

L

Good luck

When luck arrived, it broke open the door.

He slept and awoke as a prince.
[Of the newly rich.]

Throw the lucky one into the sea, and he will come out with a fish in his mouth.

Her sun shines at night.

Hey! Your beard is dipped in oil today!
[You're lucky today!]

We asked for it from the heavens: we found it on earth.

Some sleep whilst their luck is awake.

If time is on your side, cleanse your house with 'head-clay', polish it with olive oil, and raise your bed and sleep on your good luck.
[In short, enjoy your good life. 'Head-clay' is a

certain reddish, soft earth (locally called Tteen-khawa) which, moistened with water, is used by women for washing their hair.]

When winds of good luck blow they blow through all cracks.

They who have luck find the winds bringing their firewood in.

Luck's ups and downs

Your first luck is a song, your second is an everyday melody.

Luck is like a bath-house basin: empty and full, full and empty.
– TURKISH

One pail of mud, another of water.

Your luck may get sick, but it doesn't die.

If luck knocks at your door open it, and if luck quits, see it off.

If your wind blows, winnow.

Luck comes like a turtle and goes like a gazelle.

Luck is the daydream of the idle.
– PERSIAN

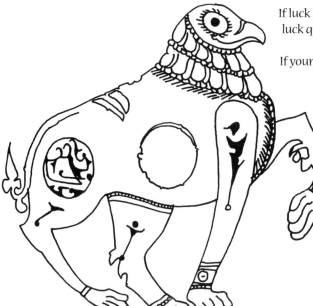

LYING

He kept telling his lie until he believed himself.

If a liar tells you the milk is white, don't believe her.

When he found his own lie spreading in the market place, he started to believe it.
– PERSIAN

Lies are the salt of people.
– PERSIAN
[They add taste to their words.]

The grip of lying
A man came to the Prophet asking him for counsel on how to give up three vices which seemed to be persistent with him, namely adultery, stealing and lying.
'Stop lying and the other vices will vanish on their own,' counseled the Prophet.
'How is that, O apostle of God?' asked the sinner.
   'If you take up saying the truth, you will then have to tell your household whom you have been with, or where you have got the stolen things from,' expounded the Prophet.

The liar's late mother was a virgin.

The palm of lying may grow short-lived flowers, but no fruit.
– TURKISH

Truth constructs, lies make ruins.

Follow a liar to the door of her house.
[Check on the spot on what she says.]

Only a liar needs to swear.

Like a dagger without a hilt, a liar's word cuts his own hand.

A liar's candle keeps burning until someone casts a look into it.

A useful lie is better than a harmful truth.
– PERSIAN

Poor liar! He is charged with many a lie, which he has never heard of.

Other than my father and mother, everybody lies.

M

Seventy gates are open to the house of madness.

Explain to the madman and he will understand; explain to a fool and he won't.

The thread between the mad and the wise can't be cut off.

Saved by madness
The story goes that a madman went up a minaret with a kidnapped child and threatened to throw it down to the ground. By chance another madman was passing by and was asked for help. 'Hey, you up there! Come down with that child, or else... I'll cut the minaret down,' he called out to him, and the madman came down with the child.

The MARKET

MADNESS

His upper floor is rented.

A thousand minds were fetched for the madwoman, yet she liked her own the best.

A madman threw a rock into the well, and it took a thousand wise people to take it out.

First give him a mind and then take him to task.

The wise person pauses, the madwoman crosses the river.

Madness of the world is shared by the whole world.
[Not quite equally, though.]

Count the rotten ones before the sound ones.
[A shrewd merchant foresees loss before profit.]

To miss a bargain is to miss a mishap.
[Think twice about a 'bargain'.]

Be friends like brothers, but deal like strangers.

He sold wheat and delivered barley.

Buy as if you were to sell.
[Buy something you could later on sell, if the need should arise.]

Look as I look!
['Buy at your risk!' – A vendor to the buyer, thus declining any responsibility for faulty goods after sale.]

Too much talk won't make it cheaper.

M

To keep your capital safe is half the profit.
Don't buy a thing you don't need, or you can't
buy things you do.
– TURKISH

The big monkey is for fifty, and the small
monkey is for fifty.
[It remains up to the buyers to see for themselves what
makes the difference.]

'Good, cheap and of a good origin' is a bargain
that never was.

First look at the nape, then take the shot at it!
[See first how much the would-be buyer can pay, then
quote the 'right price!']

Sallim, ballim! – IRAQI
[Put your cash down and (then) load your boat!]

Give credit and lose your goods, ask for
payment and get an enemy.

Ah, take the cash and let the credit go!
– OMAR KHAYYAM (1048 - 1131), Persian
mathematician, astronomer and poet

Bahlool was asked why he bought five eggs
for two piasters and sold seven eggs for two. 'I
want to be called a trader,' he replied.

If tastes were alike, goods would age in
shops.

Gold is polished with bran.

Business doesn't mix with astrology.
A vinegar seller can't stand another vinegar
seller.

Goods carried around will sell cheap; goods
staying at home will be dear.
[Advice to hoard.]

Come in as a looker (window-shopper) and go
out as a buyer.

Musk may sell for the price of weeds.

In business there is no friendship.

It is better to sell and repent than not to sell
and repent.

The shop is yours!
['And the price is mine!' – A shopkeeper's 'welcoming'
gesture to the customer.]

He sells medicine for (curing) death, don't you
know?
[His prices are sky high.]

Leave the honey in the jar till the market is
ajar.

'Cheap' is expensive even if made cheaper.

Sell with a smile and buy with a frown.

'Cheap' is not without a fault; 'dear' is not without value.

The trader with barley has no sacks, the trader with sacks has no barley.

He who knows loss won't miss profit.

From a bad debtor take (even) a handful of earth.

The cow merchant knows the sheep merchant.

A merchant doesn't exchange eggs for eggs.

What is traded in consent makes everybody content.

If the market warms up, slaughter your dog for it.

When you're in the market, buy and sell; and when you're with your companions dance and sing.

Knives are sharpened at the shop's doors!
[This is to denounce soaring prices, with shopkeepers cast in the role of 'butchers' of people's pockets.]

Be fair to a buyer, even if he were the mayor.

He sold fish still swimming in the river.

Business does not mix with astrology.

The mosque preaches honesty, the marketplace teaches fraud.

MARRIAGE

A hasty marriage is a slow sorrow.

Marriage is for pleasure; divorce when thinking it over.
– SUMERIAN

Hold on to your monkey, lest you get more of a monkey.

If you want to take a monkey for fortune, the fortune will (some day) go and the monkey will stay.
[OR: He who married for money only made a deal.]

Had the sword married, it would have become blunt.

The first spouse is sugar, the second is bitter, and the third will take you for a stroll in Heaven.

The beginning was sweet, the end was bitter.

When an old man takes a young wife, the youth of the neighborhood will rejoice.

I was married in order to get a new dress, but got my face stained and got into in a mess.
[By an unlucky wife.]

Marriage is like a castle under siege: those within want to get out, those outside want to get in.
– PERSIAN

Marry and grow tame.
– ANDALUSIAN

First marriage, then pilgrimage.

Rather marry the foolish daughter of a wise

mother than the wise daughter of a foolish mother.
[Of the mother's influence.]

They have put the cheese on their bread.
– LEVANTINE
[They have just married.]

'My sister's wedding is a double pleasure for me!'
[First, out of gladness for her sister. Second, the older sister's marriage will allow the younger one her turn, for it is customary that sisters ought to marry in order of age.]

Choose your horse with your eyes and your spouse with your ears.
[Hear what others say of her or him.]

Go and find yourself a man in the market place, rather than seek him in your cupboard at home.

It is better to marry someone who loves you than someone you love.
– PERSIAN

'It was my good luck!' said the one who was lucky in marriage; 'It was my parents who blighted my life!' said the unlucky one.
[Parents traditionally help in fixing marriages, and so they are often exposed to blame for ill luck in their children's marriages.]

If you see a couple in harmony, know that one of them is bearing the other.

Look into the roots before you plant it in your garden.
[Look into the family background first.]

A man's heart is like a cabbage: he gives its leaves away one by one, but he keeps the core for his wife.

M

Tests of the groom

There is an anecdote of a man who stole a bull and made a banquet with its meat for its owner. This curious sequence of events refers to an ancient tribal practise which tolerated a young man 'stealing' a camel, horse or cow, after warning their owner. This was seen as proof of his virility and courage when he wished to prove himself a suitable match for a would-be bride. And so the suitor of the anecdote must have managed – not entirely without the covert help of the potential bride from inside the household – to 'steal' their bull and invite his future father-in-law to a banquet to tell him: 'Here is the meat of your bull, help yourself to it!' In this manner he won the hand of his chosen bride.

* * *

A custom of the Levant requires a suitor to prove himself fit by lifting for an appropriate number of times a heavy stone-roller which has a wooden grip fixed inside (usually available in village public squares). Or he should pull the church bell's cord sixteen times continuously before coming to ask the hand of his would-be bride. Expressions such as 'He did lift the roller!' or 'He did pull the bell cord!' humorously imply that a man is 'fit' for the woman in question.

Shan and Tabaqa

The story goes that a Bedouin, Shan, met a traveler on a trip, and gave him a lift on the back of his camel. As they rode on, Shan turned to his companion and asked him:

'Would you like to carry me, or should I carry you, fellow-traveler?' The man was amazed, as they were both already riding. They then passed a field, and the host asked his guest whether the field was green or already dry. A queer question, thought his co-traveler, for the field was high and thriving. Nearing the end of their journey, they passed a funeral procession, and Shan once more presented his co-rider with another strange question, asking him whether the person inside the coffin was dead or alive.

When the puzzled traveler arrived home, he told his daughter, Tabaqa, of the curious conversation he had had with his comrade of the road. Tabaqa pondered for a while and said to him: 'Your companion put witty questions indeed to you, father.' He was all ears to hear what she meant.

'From whether he should carry you or you him, he wanted to know whether you preferred to entertain him, or he you on the way,' explained Tabaqa.

'As to whether the field was green or it had dried up already, he just wondered whether the owner had already sold the crops and spent the price in advance, or not yet.

'And as for his query about the person inside the coffin, he was curious whether the dead one had left good deeds or a thriving family behind who would keep their name alive or not.'

The man then hurried to Shan to answer his questions. Shan, wanting to know who had provided him the right answers, eventually went to Tabaqa and married her.

Today the saying goes 'Shan and Tabaqa were well-matched', implying full harmony between two persons, especially with respect to their characters and purpose.

The Dahha dance

In order to ensure that a couple enjoys the freedom of choice when it comes to marriage, the custom with some Bedouin peoples demands that the bride and groom perform a duel-dance at the feast on the eve of the wedding, each with a sword or dagger in hand. Presumably, the custom entitles either of them to use the weapon to attempt to warn the other of rejection even at this late stage. The proposal would then be rendered null and void, yet the engagement presents would be retained. This of course doesn't often take place, but the custom of the Dahha dance is upheld as a symbol of freedom of choice in marriage partners.

MARTYR

It's the cause not the death that makes a martyr.

The ink of scholars is more sacred than the blood of the martyrs.
– HADITH

MATCH

It is good that a patch be of the same color as the garment.

These belong to those, and here we are: we belong together.

MEALS

The stomach is not a storeroom.

There will be someone for every meal.

Breakfast is the rivet of the body.
– KURDISH

Eat when hungry and cease before you are sated.
– HADITH

Talking at meals brings devils to the table.

There's a meal you eat and another that eats you.
[OR: One meal could spoil others yet to come.]

When the mouth is open the eyes are closed.

Have lunch and have a nap, dine and have a walk.

To eat on a full stomach is to dig a grave for oneself.
– TURKISH

Eat alone and cough alone.
[The self-centered person will suffer alone.]

When the belly is empty, the body becomes

M

MEANNESS

When a mean wretch cannot vie with you
in virtue,
Out of his wretchedness he begins to
slander you.
– SHEIKH SADI, thirteenth century Persian Sufi
poet

'After my donkey, let no grass grow any
longer.'

'I've fattened you – I haven't eaten you, alas!'

Count your fingers as you shake hands with
him!

If you plant sweet basil in the mean person's
plot, you will reap but thorns.
– KURDISH

He wouldn't piss on a wounded one's hand.

'I've had my fill already – stop eating!'

'I've no mercy for you, I won't let anyone show
you mercy, nor will I let
God's mercy befall you.'

To rejoice at others'
misfortunes is but
meanness.

Don't untie a bundle of
radishes, don't break a
loaf of bread and don't
lift a jug of water, yet help yourself until
you've had your fill.
[The mean person's 'invitation'.]

Mean spirits readily collapse under
frustration.
– Lilminber

spirit, and when it is full, the spirit becomes
body.
– SHEIKH SADI, thirteenth century Persian Sufi
poet

Wear what covers and eat what nourishes.

The first plate is for hunger, the second for
nourishment, and the third for stomach
trouble.

Meals first, then prayers.
– NAJDI

The stomach is the house of illness.

Bahlool and the glutton
Bahlool happened to attend a banquet one
day, where he noticed a man eating
greedily and filling his pockets with food
as he did so. He then took a jug of water
and poured it into the man's pocket,
saying: 'Sir, I see that your pockets have
eaten so much that they must now be
thirsty!'

The MEANS

If you don't have wings, how can you fly; if you don't have legs how can you walk?
– SUMERIAN

Do you want pearls? Go then and dive into the sea. Do you want a bride? Go and get silver.

The one without a spoon will burn her fingers.
[BUT: Your hand is your mother, the spoon is your stepmother.]

He lost the keys before he lost the way.

A well can't be filled with dew.

If you don't have a camel, charge your ox and trust it to God.

Hold onto your dog's tail till you have crossed the river.

Why burn the eiderdown to kill a flea?!
– TURKISH

If you take care of your donkey, it will take you to Mecca.
– MOROCCAN
[Morocco is a good distance from the holy city of Mecca.]

He was baking a loaf on a cloud of smoke.

If you can't enter by the door of love, try the door of silver.

A jar that has two ears can be carried by two hands.

Nail can pull up nail.

For every beard there is a fit pair of scissors.

Fit the gown to your measurements, not the measurements to your gown.

MEDIATOR

A mediator is to get a stick or two.
[Someone attempting to mediate during a quarrel will also receive blows.]

Go between two foes in such a way that once they are reconciled you won't lose face with either.
– PERSIAN

MEDICINE

Medicine is bitter, recovery is sweet.

A gold ring can't heal a broken finger.

An hour in pain, rather than (pain) every hour.

A scorpion is in the sleeve, (whilst) the doctor

is (still) in Baghdad!
[Obviously, an old saying of the Levant when Baghdad used to be the center of the prosperous Middle East.]

A doctor's miss is Fate's hit.

Here is your medicine, yet with God lies your recovery!

The medicine that heals all illness is time.

MEETING

Mountains don't meet, faces do.

The living may meet the living.

Meet a person with open hand, and they'll meet you with open heart.

Away with his statue, let us meet the man!

He who wants to meet the waterman should seek him in autumn.
– MOROCCAN
[The waterman goes around houses selling water in water-skins during summer-time; in autumn when it rains he can be found at home. This proverb counsels meeting people at a time that is right for them.]

MEN

Were I the sun, I wouldn't rise on a short man!

A tall man is not the one who (necessarily) can support a wall, nor is a short one the one who can dig a tunnel.

Short men are flaring brands.
[That is, they are intelligent and active.]

Whilst a short man scratched his head, a tall man ate figs.
– MOROCCAN

One could enter a lion's heart before (trying) the heart of a man.

Some men are like pumpkins: the older they are, the lighter (their minds).

It is just like a man: nothing straight about it!

Men go to the victor.

Every man carries his own devil under his own armpit.

Beware! I told you, he was a man!

He has neither riches to lose to the Sultan, nor a mind to Satan.

Men are wicked in each others' opinions.

M

God created man and repented!
[Said as a reproach to wickedness.]

Man prays for evil, as he prays for good, and man was ever in haste.
– THE QUR'AN

Men are hidden under their tongues.

Don't laud a gown before you have it on, nor a man before you prove him.

A great man does not know it, the not-so-great one is known to nobody.
– TURKISH

A man is as big as his two smaller limbs: his heart and his tongue.
[In Arabic culture the 'heart' actually connotes the 'mind'.]

Some men are good for the sword, some for hospitality, some for wisdom and guidance, and some are good for nothing.

The older a man, the bigger his aspirations.

Women have two tricks, men have one.

Every man is a boy in his own home.

A man under duress should be like the lower millstone: ever stable and firm.
– KURDISH
[OR: A man should be like tea: its strength shows only in boiling water. – AFGHAN]

God created men to lay barley for the donkeys.
– KURDISH

Women ask, men answer.

Men are birds without wings.

Man is harder than steel, more closed than rocks and more tender than flowers.

A man is not the one who reaches his goal, but the one who goes for it.

Men are earners, women are builders (of homes).

The original man would eat long beans, rather than resort to underhand means.
[Long beans are the 'poor person's' dish in Egypt.]

Rich men are like black sultanas: they sweeten one's mouth, they make time pass sweetly, and they make one's bowels 'run' swiftly too.

A trader would offer his goods; a man, himself.
– Lilminber

> ## Worthy men
> Men worthy of tears and lamentations are of three kinds: a man who is ready to face peril to put out the flames of war; a man who entertains his guests in famine years and offers them water in days of thirst; and a man of spirit and intelligence who, with the power of his mind and eloquence, is able to secure his own rights and defends others'. The rest are not men but males who can only multiply their own kind of mortals. They deserve no tears nor mourning, and a blind person who cannot have a look at them will miss nothing worth seeing.
> – JAZIA AL-HILALAITE, Bedouin poet of the Maghreb

Of three things a man has more than he knows: of sins, of debts and of foes.

God desires to make your burden light for you, for man has been created weak.
– THE QUR'AN

MESSENGER

Send a keen messenger and she will render the message to your satisfaction.

Were you not a messenger, I would have cut off that which holds your eyes!
[That is: 'your head' – a ruler to a defiant messenger.]

Three (things) show who you are: your friend, your book and your messenger.

MIDDLE PATH

Good is to be found between two evils.
[That is, between two extremes.]

That which bends won't break.

Be not dry lest you break, nor be too soft lest you be squeezed.

And let not your hands be chained to your neck, nor stretch it out all the way.
– THE QUR'AN

MIND

Two hands are no good without one head.

A man of the mind beats a man of the sword.

The mind is a gift from God, knowledge is the gift of the mind.

The eye is for seeing, the heart is for believing. [It was believed the heart was the center of mind.]

Some minds are as big as two walnuts rattling together in an empty sack.

Knowledge comes from school, character comes from home.

The heart shows the direction, the mind shows the way. – Lilminber

Mind and morality are indispensable partners – if they don't work together, they destroy each other.
– Lilminber

No one saw God with their eyes!
[One should also use the mind's reasoning.]

If your mind is not with you, you won't find it anywhere you go.

If you want to have peace of mind, keep saying: Never mind!

Ask not of someone's mind, what is in yours about theirs should suffice.

MISER

Like a grave, the miser gives nothing back.

For fear of poverty, a miser lives in it already.

It was neither for himself, nor for his dog.

If a miser ever thought to give something, Heaven's angels would open their eyes.

Silver doesn't belong to the miser, but the miser belongs to silver.

The miser would like to hide death inside a jar.
[She is too mean even to give death away.]

Her tongue is (sweet) dates, but her hands are (dry) wood.

He was too mean to wish (God's) mercy for the dead.

The miser's hand stuck in boiling water.

Tell the miser: his fortunes will either stray through hazards or will end up with heirs.

The miser eventually is a keen servant.

A thousand times 'Miser!' rather than once 'Needy!'
[A miser answers back.]

Miserliness is a branch of Zaqqoom!
[Zaqqoom is the 'Tree of Fire' in Hell, so misers are sinners.]

I am not a miser, but have nothing to give.

Not for that worthless one a prayer afford,
Who life in hoarding spent – never spent his hoard.
– SHEIKH SADI, thirteenth century Persian Sufi poet

A child is born with hands closed,
Telling of man's absurd miserliness;
Look at him leaving with open hands,
Betraying himself as bare and penniless.
– ABUL ALAA AL-MA'ARRI, eleventh century poet

MISHAPS

A thousand sips cannot replace one choking.

If you want to bear a mishap lightly, forget about it.
[OR: Away with the broom and its litter into the sea! – MOROCCAN]

MOCKERY

He who jeers will dance without a tamborine.
[He will amuse no one.]

Those who have indulged themselves in ridicule will on Doomsday be called to the door of Paradise and have it shut in their face.
– HADITH

MONEY

'Floos w-namoos' – Money and honor?!
[How could they go together?]

Bad money serves bad ends.
[ALSO: From his hand to Satan's mouth!]

Money is the dust in the mansion of the world.

Stolen money walks in the dark.

She who seeks money in halal (legal) ways is like the one who tries to hold water in a sieve.

The ashtray and the rich: the fuller they are, the dirtier.

If you want to know the effect of money on its holders look at the faces of the rich.

Money summons the genie.

If you don't have money at your home, go and fetch it with your teeth.

Money strays, and people bring it back home.
[By working.]

Work in mud and eat out of it.

M

It is inscribed on the face of coins: Fulfillers of Needs.

If you want to have a cold drink in Hell, don't forget to enter it with some coins in your pocket.

Your ally is your purse, and the rial is your cousin.
[The rial is the currency unit of Saudi Arabia.]

Dirhams are sweet balm.
– IRAQI
[A dirham was a small silver coin, one-twentieth the value of a dinar in Iraq.]

From a friend or from an enemy, dirhams are money.
– IRAQI

It is the eye and the ear, it is the hands and the feet.

The piaster taught its owner to speak seven languages.
[A piaster is one-hundredth of a Jordanian dinar.]

Money can build a road inside the sea.

Nothing can cut off a hand of gold.
– TURKISH

Money is like a rose; smell it and pass it on to the next person.

If you put coins over your head you will look small, but if you put them under your feet you will be raised high.

Men gain money and money gains men.

If money is in your pocket, it is your servant; if not, you are its servant.

Bedouin riches
A Bedouin of old was asked: 'Which riches are the best?'
   'A brown date-palm in a fertile soil, a yellow camel in a green pasture and a flowing fountain in a yielding land,' replied the Bedouin.
   'What about gold and silver, then?'
   'What is a wise person to do with them? Two stones jingling together – if you approach them, they'll disappear, and if you keep them they won't grow.'

Money is a horseman.
[One needs to run fast after it.]

A sword of silver can cut a sword of steel. – PERSIAN

Fire tests gold and gold tests the kadi (judge).

Money is a bird: it builds its nest in a safe place.

Health without fortune is an illness without pain.

Gold is a yellowish dust without a tongue, but once it speaks out all listen.

Don't yearn for money, learn to count.

Wealth and children are the ornament of this world.
– THE QUR'AN

MORNING

If cocks fight at night, the morning will come late.

The cat jumps, the cock crows, the sleeper awakens, and here comes the morning.
– KURDISH

One is more ready to face a bad morning than to enjoy a good evening.

MOUNT

You may serve three without shame: your household, your guest and your mount.

A donkey was invited to a wedding party. 'Is it in order to carry water or to fetch firewood from the forest?' it wondered.

MOURNING

A mourning soul sheds tears for all the sorrowful.

The bereaved are kin.

All things start small and grow big, except sorrow.

If your bosom feels depressed, go and visit the graveyard.
– HADITH

MYSTERY

The riddle was covered by an onion-peel.
[It appeared so plain and obvious.]

My father was a merchant of dust, and so he is gone with the wind.

There was the Door to which I found no key
There was the Veil through which I might
not see.
– OMAR KHAYYAM (1048 - 1131), Persian mathematician, astronomer and poet.

Mysteries are the host of knowledge.
– Lilminber

Ten weavers are busy down at the looms, yet the name belongs to the House.

can one do but ride them?

Lacking horses, one had to saddle the dogs.
[The meaning is metaphorical: the horse implies a brave and able person, the dog the contrary.]

Necessities have their own judges and juries.

NEED

Spend your night without broth and you will wake up without faith.

It also happened that a lion followed a fox to pick up bones after it.

Someone sold their son out of need, another bought him on credit.

The one who needs fire will hold it in her own hand.

Fear of need is a need itself.

The thirsty goat breaks the jar.

She who had salty cheese for her meal will know how to find her way to the water.
– TURKISH

It is good to help others, but it is still better not to be in need of their help.

'What does my naked slave want?'
'A ring for my finger, Sir!'

NAME

A good name is better than a pretty face.

A good name will not die; a bad name is already dead.

If you are called harvester, sharpen your sickle.

NECESSITY

He who falls in the river will cling to the snake's tail.

If there is nothing to mount but spears, what

He smells his hand and tells himself he has had his fill.
[Rather than asking for a meal.]

The tribe is faring well: only garments and food are missing.

'Don't cry, my child; your eye has become as big as an egg.'
'And that is what I want, mother!'

NEIGHBORS

Shut your door and trust your neighbor.

A bad neighbor sees what enters, not what goes out.
[That is: they only notice their neighbor's faults or perhaps their income – what enters – and not their virtues or assets – what goes out.]

If your neighbor didn't look at your face, she would look at your backside.

Love your neighbor but don't let him enter your house.

Oppose your ruler, not your neighbor.

Be friends, not neighbors.
[OR: Distance from people is gain.]

If your neighbor makes a pilgrimage (to holy Mecca) once, watch him; if twice shun him; and if thrice move to another house.

We didn't sell the house, we sold the neighbor.

'Our loaves are bigger than yours!'
'Give us some then, O good neighbor!'

I am talking to you, O my daughter-in-law, but listen, you there behind the wall.
[A reproach to a nosy neighbor.]

True, I may be from neighbor's eye concealed:
God knows my acts, both secret and
                    revealed.
– SHEIKH SADI, thirteenth century Persian Sufi poet

Seek a comrade for the road and a neighbor for the house.

Give loaf and take loaf; but don't let your neighbor stay aloof.

Lean towards your nearby neighbor, rather than your faraway brother.

Don't covet your neighbor's house; yours will then remain safe.

Betray your neighbor, but ask no counsel from anyone!
[You will be ostracized.]

Your neighbor, your neighbor, your neighbor, then your brother!
– HADITH

Mine and my neighbor's are on fire,
And from me to him goes the hot bowl.
– From an old poem

NEWS

Don't buy moonlight or the news.
[They are both free.]

If you want to uncover the latest news shake the dust off your guest's shoulders.
[ALSO: Latecomers bring the latest news.]

When the messenger is slow, the news is good.

Glad tidings send out their joy from afar.

No spit under stone will remain covered.

If the rich person is pricked by a thorn, everyone will know it; but not if a poor one is bitten by a snake.

The distance to truth is four fingers long.
[That is, between the hearing ears and seeing eyes.]

Don't believe what you hear, nor all what you see.
– BEDOUIN

Shared secrets are public news.

That remains secret which never was.

The joy is yours, and the prize for the glad tidings is mine!
– IRAQI
[It is customary for the one who breaks good news, like the birth of a baby or safe return from a long journey, to be rewarded with a gift, 'Bishara'.]

NIGHT

Nights are the cradle of lovers' secrets, the cover of villains and the home of the good.
– PERSIAN

The day has eyes, the night has ears.

Who ever knew a night without a morning?

A long night stimulates many a song.
– IRAQI
[Starry, summer nights when a cool breeze brings relief after a long, hot day are often accompanied by merrymaking in Iraq. However, the saying also implies that events only take shape when the right circumstances arise.]

He has appointed the night as a cloak, and the day for livelihood. He is the Lord of the black night and the white day.
– THE QUR'AN

NOBILITY

Doing good is true nobility.

N

The shadow of a noble man is large.
[A noble man's 'shadow' implies his generosity, bravery and wisdom, which is what it takes to lead the tribe.]

A noble person's hand is a (just) balance.

Each knot can be untied by a noble person.
['Knot' here implies a problem or predicament.]

NOISE

Fear constant noise as much as the Angel of Death.

A crying cat catches no rat.

NOSINESS

She can hear the breathing of ants.

Whilst the inquisitive one was set on fire, he noticed the wood was greenish.

He is asking who the father of the bastard is.

Someone wore a beard, another felt it tickling.

She who looks above her head will have a sore neck.

The nosy dog makes a good sentry.

You who intrude between the fingernail and the skin will only get the rot therein.

The stone that doesn't lie in your way need not break your toes.
[OR: Curiosity killed the cat.]

He who digs up his mother's history might not hear good news.

O

The obstinate one does not hold an opinion, the opinion holds him.
— SHEIKH SADI, thirteenth century Persian Sufi poet

Obedience without faith is slavery.
— Lilminber

To disobey an oppressor is obedience to God.
— HADITH

And on Doomsday, they shall say: O our Lord, we obeyed our chiefs and great ones, and they led us away from the right path.
— THE QUR'AN

OBSTINACY

Cooked together with him in the pot, a stone was ready first.
— AFGHAN

The obstinate one has no answer.

OFFENSE

An offense by one villain may injure a million.

OBEDIENCE

If you want to be obeyed, ask for what is plausible.

You must obey those you wish to serve.

If someone doesn't hear with their ears, let them hear with their nape.
[Take a shot at them.]

They who can't obey, can't command.

If you must eat pork, ensure it is fatty.
— TURKISH
[Pork is forbidden in Islam. 'Fatty' here means wholesome and tasty.]

If you want to commit an offense, make it big.
— PERSIAN

If injury is added to insult, it will be a complete offense.
— PERSIAN

OFFICE

An office is as big as the person.

OLD-FASHIONED

Old-fashioned women feel insulted when offered some wine; their modern daughters swallow the insult.
– EGYPTIAN

OMENS

Take omens from the mouths of children.

Slow news bodes well.

Eat, Drink, Wear and Go Broke
This is a superstitious chant from old Aleppo used when going to rent a house. As ceilings consisted of tree trunks laid down one beside the other, a would-be tenant would come and start counting the trunks one by one uttering the chant, a phrase, at each trunk. If the phrase 'Go broke' fell upon the last trunk, that would be inauspicious and the person would not take the house.

A mountain goat is more knowledgeable than a city soothsayer!
– KURDISH

The ill-omened one brings bad luck, even if you put a lantern on his head.
– LEVANTINE
['Lantern' here alludes to light, connoting good omens.]

In a bad year, the she-goat mounts the male.

OPPORTUNITY

If heaven rains dates, open your mouth.
– PERSIAN

Opportunities pass quickly and return slowly.

If your wind blows, winnow your threshing floor.

When the stream flows, frogs start singing songs.

OPPRESSION

In time the house of the oppressor is ruined.

The oppressed one's day with the oppressor will be longer than the oppressor's with the oppressed.
– HADITH

Oppression cannot last too long, otherwise it'll ruin the world.

Oppression and the plague
An oppressive ruler of old once boasted to his subjects that, by his assuming reign over the kingdom, signs of plague – which had been spreading at that time – had disappeared. A member of the audience, however, stood up and said: 'God forbid, Sire, that we should have both of you together!'

Salt was ground on his back.
[He suffered a lot.]

The humility of the helpless scorns the arrogance of oppressor.
– SHEIKH SADI, thirteenth century Persian Sufi poet

No one can pick good fruit from the tree of oppression.

He who plays host to the wolf wrongs the sheep.

The oxen shed their yokes and broke loose in an uproar.
[Of the oppressed rioting.]

Every oppressor will some day meet with an oppressor of their own.

Equality in oppression is the oppressor's justice.

He who wields the sword of oppression will be slain with it.

Oppressive rule is better than constant sedition.

Lo! We have prepared for the oppressors the fire of Hell whose tent will enclose them; and if they cry for mercy, they will be relieved with water like molten lead showered to toast their faces.
– THE QUR'AN

OUTCOME

Don't utter 'Broad beans' before they are in your storeroom.
– EGYPTIAN
[The English variant is: Don't count your chickens before they are hatched.]

After fire, ashes; after rain, flowers.

Those who plant thorns won't get grapes.

OWNERSHIP

The fox pissed in the sea and said: 'This is mine.'

You hold on to your hens and I'll hold on to my cocks.

He who owns the ear of a camel has the right to make it kneel.

The donkey is mine and I ride it howsoever I like.

People don't ask what you spent, but what you have got.

Better to say 'Here it is' than 'Here it was'.

What is here is mine, what is there is ours!

A castle-owner wondered if he could build for himself a castle in Paradise as well. 'You can,' one said to him, 'if you give up your castle on earth.'

A landlord has one house, a tenant has a thousand.

A thousand cranes in the air are not worth one sparrow in the hand.

They who earn get much, they who save get more.
– PERSIAN

What you own is what you have eaten which has already perished; what you have put on is what you have worn out; but what you have offered of charity is that which you have indeed saved.
– HADITH

Unto God belong the easts and the wests.
– THE QUR'AN

P

There is misery in hell and happiness in paradise, but on earth there are both.
– TURKISH

PARADISE

'How far is it between myself and paradise?'
'Lift your head and see!'

Paradise must be a fine place, no doubt, but one has to squeeze one's heart to reach it.
– AFGHAN

Paradise without people is not a nice place.

Paradise is for those who control their anger.
– HADITH

PARENTS

Blessed is the home that begets another.

After my parents, relatives are (just) neighbors.

Warrants are by parents.

Parents' ire is a debt.
[One has to redeem oneself to them.]

A person without a child has a hole in their heart; a person with children has a heart like a sieve.

A crow asked who the prettiest bird was pointed to its child.
[The crow is traditionally associated with bad luck.]

Father's stick hurts, mother's hand heals.

The mother of the dead can sleep, but not the mother of the wounded.

Even if the sun shines all day and the lamp burns all night, a house without a mother is dark.

When your son grows a beard, shave yours off.
[The beard used to be a symbol of manhood and prestige. This saying implies that when the son grows up, his father is to relinquish his responsibilities to him.]

Father is a little god.

116

P

A father bore many a child, many a child could not bear a father.

Daddy is dead, and we have run out of flour.

Father's friend is the son's uncle.

The dead father's eye is large.
[His children will become ever more aware of their father's counsels and approach to life.]

Children of the mustaches are raised by the beard; children of the beard, by the gray hair; and children of the gray hair are raised as orphans.

The eye of the father is on his son; the eye of the son is on the stone.
[That is, on the gravestone, thus 'waiting' for his father's death in order to inherit.]

If the father eats too much salt in his life, the son will die of thirst.
['Too much salt' implies too many sins or blunders.]

My son is a rogue, yes, but I don't like to hear it from anyone else.

His father was garlic and his mother was onion: how could he then become rose-jam?

The rogue and the daughter's father are not good friends.

With the arrival of the stepmother, the father becomes a stepfather.
– AFGHAN

PARTNER

A thousand squandering monkeys rather than one suspicious partner.

'O, my partner, God bless you!'
'Yours is half the blessing for sure, partner!'

'God willing, we will recover what is lost!'
'God willing, we will retain what is left,' responded the partner.

If there were a shared face, no one would wash it.

A donkey of your own is better than a shared thoroughbred mare.

The pot of partnership was cooked but never eaten.

The PAST

You are the child of your past.

What is past is an image, what is to come is a wish. You have only this hour – take it.

Squeeze the past like a sponge, smell the present like a rose and send a kiss to the future.

P

Now that the pumpkin is large and round, it has forgotten about its past.

Call yesterday back if you can,
No king can do it nor sultan.
– ABUL ALAA AL-MA'ARRI, eleventh century poet

PASTIME

The soul is green and the time is springtime!

Take a good hour to redeem a thousand foul ones.

Youth, fortunes and leisure spoil a person beyond measure.

PATIENCE

The medicine of the times is patience.
Patience is the key to success.

Haste brings forth failure.

Patience heals the broken bone.

God created heavens in seven days!
[Be patient!]

He dug a well with a needle.

Patience is absence, longing is presence.
[This refers to patience and absence in terms of one's heart's desire.]

Patience extracts acid from the sweet.
[OR: It is with patience that the orchard turns into jam. – TURKISH]

Patience cures all hardships save folly.

It was with patience that the camel rode the ant.

The door of patience needs no doorman.

Patience is of two kinds: one is to bear what one does not desire, and the other is to sustain missing what one desires. Both show courage.
– IMAM ALI, seventh century, the fourth Khalif of Islam

Better be patient with yourself than let others be patient with you.

If meat is dear, patience is cheap.

Patience is a tree whose root is bitter, but whose fruit is sweet.

Patience is strength for the weak, impatience is weakness for the strong.

Patience can move mountains.

Long patience may reach the grave.
[OR: She was patient until a palm-tree grew on her head.]

PEACE

You go and take your enemy's land, the enemy comes and takes yours.
– SUMERIAN

Peace with fear is no peace.

Eating stones in a peaceful land is healthy.

The tree of silence bears the fruit of peace.

They who do not find peace at home are already at war.

'I challenge you to a duel.'
'I challenge you to go in peace.'

Peace stays with conditions fulfilled.

'Salamun aleykun!'
['Peace be upon you' – the daily greeting]

Peace with sword in hand is war.

Reply not roughly to smooth language, nor Contend with him who knocks at peace's door.
– SHEIKH SADI, thirteenth century Persian Sufi poet

The world is wide for those who live in peace, narrow for those who quarrel.
– UZBEK

PEOPLE

When people talk, they talk about things they don't know.

She who weeps for all people, her eyes will end up blind.

People are locks, for each there is a unique key.

People are soldiers, some fight together, some fight one another.

People follow the victor.

People are more like their times than their parents.

People are enemies of what they ignore.

Serve people but don't ask them for thanks.

Our real tombs are not in the ground but in people's hearts.
– TURKISH

Just like people, and that is fine.

People are kinsfolk, yet different in character.

People's company

I took up with people for forty years; they did not forgive me a slip, nor cover me for a fault, nor keep a secret for me. None had compassion for my tears, none fulfilled a need for me, none accepted an excuse from me, and none set me right after failure. None of them missed me in my absence, and none cared much for my presence.
– An ancient author

If people tell you your head is missing, touch it and see.

If everybody tells you that you are an ass, thank God and bray.

People need people in winter or summer,
They are but servants to each other.

People are planks until they get acquainted.

If people lose their minds, your own won't do on its own.

If people become alike, they will become a horde.

To join people is a feast.

You are created peoples and tribes so that you make acquaintance with one another; lo! the best of you are the pious among you.
– THE QUR'AN

PERSEVERANCE

Steady drops pierce rocks.

Diligence is a good teacher.

The world is on the side of her who is left standing.
– TURKISH

PIONEER

Merit belongs to the initiator even if the successor has done still better.

The one who carries the standard must also know the way.

PLAY

Get it done, then have fun.

To play with a cat is to sustain its scratches.

Play alone rather than stay lonely.

An old bear is the plaything of its cubs.

One hour for your God, another for your heart.

PLEASURE

The tongue of a candle will laugh but not for long.

There is no pleasure without a tincture of bitterness.

When even the camels join in mirth and glee,
If men feel naught, then must they asses be.
– SHEIKH SADI, thirteenth century Persian Sufi poet

POETRY

Teach your children poetry: it opens the mind, lends grace to wisdom and makes the heroic virtues hereditary.
– Attributed to IMAM AS-SADIQ, ninth century scholar

Some poetry is wisdom, and some wisdom is poetry.
– HADITH

POLITICS

Politics has no religion.
– LEVANTINE

I will not put my sword in my whip's place, nor my whip in place of my tongue.
– MUAWIYA, seventh century ruler of Arabia

If there is a thread between me and my house I won't cut it off: if they pull I let go, if they let go I pull.
– MUAWIYA

British politics is like the wall of Hell: decorated from outside, but inside is the punishment.
– KEMAL ATATURK (1881-1938), the founder of modern Turkey

Politicians plan things no devil can think of.
– EGYPTIAN

When the Sultan dies, so do his alliances.

POSITION

A seat is as big as the sitter.

No need to push the one standing at the edge: he will soon fall of his own accord.

'Why do you cry as you soar high?'
'I fear falling down, that is why!'

Don't sit where you were told to quit.

Unable to speak up because of his mustache, and he can't speak down because of the beard.
[Metaphorically implied to denote the dilemma of one's critical position.]

P

POVERTY

Poverty is a gown of fire.

A poor person's door need not be locked.

A poor man in a hurry must be on his way to serve a rich man.

Nothing at hand, nothing on the shelf.

The rich are surfeited because the poor are not sated.

The funeral of a rich person and a poor person's wedding are crowded.

A poor man married a poor woman, and in a year they had a poor thing.

If your father left you poor, buy yourself a cow and sow barley.

If a poor person is ever happy, heaven's angels will be surprised.

Tears are the poor person's efforts.

P

The rich person in a foreign land is at home, the poor person at home is a stranger.

A poor person's candle!
[It serves the entire family gathering around it. Said of a small thing that is useful and pleasing.]

Whilst the tale of the rich man went on, the poor man's candle was melting away.
– LEVANTINE

The fault is in the pocket that the honor is 'pierced'.

The empty hand is dirty.
– TURKISH

When cold pays a visit to the poor person's house, it will bring illness along.

Poverty snatches the reins out of the hands of piety.
– SHEIKH SADI, thirteenth century Sufi mystic from Shiraz

Poverty is the longer death.

If the poor person sleeps on a stone pillow, the rich person sleeps on seven thorns.
[Perhaps due to the worries of their fortune.]

They who own much silver may be happy, they who own much barley may be happy, but they who own nothing can sleep.
– SUMERIAN

Would that someone, even a black crow, were indebted to me!

Give ye the poor their due when harvesting the field.
– HADITH

POWER

Power is an exhausting game.

Curse the Sultan in his absence and Satan in his presence.

One lie in the Sultan's head overshadows a thousand truths.

When the Sultan allowed the taking of ten eggs, his soldiers seized a hundred chickens.
– TURKISH

They who takes grapes from the Sultan have to give him dates.

A lord's dog is a lord of dogs.

Wield your sword and rest under its shadow.

One mat suffices for two dervishes, but a whole land can't be large enough for two chieftains.

The lion is absent and the beasts are feasting.

P

They who eat at the table of the Sultan have to fight with his sword.

The hand that you can't bite, kiss!

When the King starts to sing, his throne will start shaking under him.
– ANDALUSIAN
[Singing here implies leading a frivolous lifestyle.]

If the Devil becomes a bridge, better cross by swimming.
– KURDISH

A hand over a hand will reach the sky.

When the arm is strong, the eyes stay dry.

What does Acre care for the swell of the sea?
[Acre was a fortified port of Palestine.]

His spout pours out far and wide.
[He is generous and influential.]

O, believers, obey those in authority amongst you.
– THE QUR'AN

Oppose your minister but not his doorkeeper.

A donkey remains a donkey, even if it carries the treasury of the Sultan.

On the throne with a crown, yet in need of those who are down!

Compassion out of place spoils authority.
– SHEIKH SADI, thirteenth century Persian Sufi poet

PRAYERS

To sleep with faith is better than to pray in doubt.
– IMAM ALI, seventh century, the fourth Khalif of Islam

A wall is stronger than a hundred prayers.
[To lean on.]

A hundred pilgrimages won't fry an egg.

O, watermill! Stop turning, for you are disturbing my prayers!

Meals come before prayers.
– BEDOUIN

They who can, act; those who can't raise their hands in prayers.

The cruelest hearts are also found amongst those who do not miss their daily prayers.
– PERSIAN

Bahlool was asked which direction one should look (towards sacred Mecca) for saying the prayers whilst in the water. 'One should look towards where the clothes are,' he said.

To curse the faith when wronged by it is like saying prayers when blessed by it.
– LEVANTINE

No one will pray but in the hope of forgiveness.

O God, help us against (the temptation of) ourselves.
– From a prayer

Howsoever big the mosque is, the mullah can preach only of what he knows.

If you say your prayers amidst the sands, they will blow into your face.
– PERSIAN
[Sands here allude to sins or misdeeds.]

A saint was asked of the distance between east and west. 'A day's journey of the sun,' he said. And of the distance between earth and heaven? 'A whole-hearted prayer,' he replied.

The real mosque is built inside the soul.

All camels are marching, but ours are kneeling down!
[A complaint by perhaps a mother or housewife that whilst other men are going out in pursuit of their livelihood, hers passes his time in saying prayers at home.]

And that inverted bowl they called the sky,
Whereunder crawling coop'd we live and die;
Lift not your hand to it for help – for it
As impotently moves as you and I.
– OMAR KHAYYAM (1048-1131), Persian mathematician, astronomer and poet

PRESENTS

They who give you a rope will tie you up with it.
– PERSIAN

A present would pluck out the eye of the kadi (judge).

Feed the mouth and make the eye shy.

Benefits enslave.

Unwrapping the presents is wrapping up the friendship.
[In contrast to the custom in the West, a present is not to be unwrapped in the presence of its giver.]

The prince awarded what didn't belong to him.

A good person's present is not to be refused.

I am rich, but I like presents.

Whatever you give remains yours.
– TURKISH

P

If you receive a present on a donkey, return it on a camel.

Exchange presents and grow in friendliness.
– HADITH

PRESSURE

Milking yields milk, squeezing yields blood.

Much stretching makes loose.

PRETENSION

Either you walk like Caesar or you give up that title!
– LEVANTINE
[Walk here implies to 'behave' or 'act'.]

Enlarge your threshing floor, lest your foes gloat.

The mangy goat drinks but from the top of the fountain.

A camel was once asked its vocation. 'Silk-weaver,' it replied.
'Oh, yeah? That is quite obvious from the softness of your tender hands!'

To pretend you are rich will make you only poorer.

In daytime he is a knight and a hen at night.

Pretend to be crazy and do whatever you like.

Bahlool, the 'prophet'
Bahlool once claimed prophecy, and when people asked him for providential proof, he replied: 'What could be more provident than telling you what is in your hearts now!' They were eager to know. 'You all think I am a fake prophet, don't you?' he said.

He strolled in slippers and took himself for a nobleman.
– In ancient Aleppo
[Open-ended slippers were the footwear of the élite in times of old. ALSO: She walked in slippers and said: 'I am the servant of the élite!']

When the horse was being shod, a beetle came up and raised its feet.

PRETEXT

The camel went lame because of its ear.

The cat ate its kittens and swore they were mice.

When her arm failed her, she said she was haunted.
[Apparently, her excuse for breaking something.]

PRIESTS

The mullet, the sparrow and the mullah's son cannot be caught.

Do as I preach, not as I do.

Start your morning facing a gypsy rather than a clergyman.

The drowning mullah
The story goes that a mullah was drowning when someone passed by and offered to rescue him saying: 'Give me your hand, mullah!'.
   But before the mullah breathed his last, another passer-by also turned up and said: 'Mullah! Take my hand!' which immediately saved the drowning mullah.
   Mullahs, priests and monks are not used to giving but to taking is the moral of this tale.

Ant, snake and mullah need not worry about their livelihood.
– PERSIAN

Three things one can't see: the eye of the ant, the feet of the snake and the mullah's source of living.
– PERSIAN

PRINCE

Were we all princes, who would drive donkeys?

The prince gave of what did not belong to him!

You are a prince when you are not ruled by one.

What is right for the prince is not right for everyone.

Bad scholars are those who stand at the doors of princes, and good princes are those who stand at the scholars' doors.
– HADITH

PRIORITIES

I like you, my bracelet, but O my arm, I like you better.

Send him away like a swine, who is starved for bread but asking for wine.

She wore a fashionable yellow amber necklace standing at her demolished front door which blocked the road.

Meals first, then the prayers.

PRISON

Prison is the touchstone of one's spiritual fortitude.
– Lilminber

In prayers and in prison all are alike.
– Lilminber

Prison is for men, lamenting is for women.

The canary is a prisoner of its charming voice.

In prison one cannot go anywhere one likes; outside the prison one does not know where to go.
– MALTESE

The longest prison sentences should be reserved for the tongue.

P

PROBLEM

Go and cry at the head of the dead one.
[Don't deal with a problem before it starts to bother you.]

Shut the door through which wind enters your house.

You can't climb a mountain with a piece of gravel inside your shoe.

Healed or not healed? Or should we take him for dead?
[Wondering what has become of a long-standing problem.]

It was a summer cloud that would soon fade away.

Problems are to be met half-way and stopped from advancing further.
– Lilminber

PROMISE

Your promise is your face, and performance is its beauty.

Satan also promised Paradise to his followers.

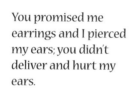

Like a summer cloud, his promise wouldn't dampen a passer-by.

You promised me earrings and I pierced my ears; you didn't deliver and hurt my ears.

His day is a month and his month is an age.

A promise without fulfillment is an assault without a sword.

Keep on living, O poor little donkey: springtime is coming soon!

Hear with pleasure, see with sorrow.

Try to touch heaven first!

People ought to stay as big as their words.

If she said: 'The house is yours,' the key would follow.
[If she promises, she will deliver.]

An egg today is better than a chicken tomorrow.

Slow down your promise, speed up your performance.

The day obliterated the promise of the night.

P

PROOF

Gold is proven by touchstone and the kadi (judge) by gold.

A thousand proofs won't prove an axiom to a fool.

If a lion is an ass, try putting a lead to its neck.

The contents of the pot are uncovered by the spoon.

'I do trust you, my Lord, yet my heart needs to be assured.'
– Prophet Ibraham asking God for a proof in THE QUR'AN

PROVERBS

Proverbs are rivets of speech.

Proverbs are the knowledge of the street.

Proverbs are short sentences edited from long experiences.
– PERSIAN

The proverb is the talking brother of silence.
– PERSIAN

PROVOCATION

Don't shake a stick in front of a shepherd.
[He is used to administering beatings.]

Hammer mud, and it will splatter you.

Stir and you will find.
[YET: Don't dig deep, lest a viper comes out for you.]

He provokes (even) the stones of the road.

PRUDENCE

Don't push your boat away after crossing a river.

Beware of still water and of the silent one.

They who plant thorns ought not to walk unshod.

A wise person won't be stung twice from the same hole.

A crow warned its son that if it saw a man bow to collect a stone, it should fly away. 'What about if he already has it under his belt?' said the little one. 'Go, my son, I am no longer worried about you,' said the parent.

A slip of the foot rather than a slip of the tongue.

P

Don't saddle a horse before it is broken in.

If you are asked whether you have seen a black donkey, say you have seen neither a black donkey nor a white donkey.

An eye on the pot, and another on the cat!

Don't stir old straw.

Don't go drinking from the Sultan's fountain.

Don't trust anyone even in the land of trust.

If you send a boy to collect grapes, follow him.

O, ye who believe! Be ever on your guard!
— THE QUR'AN

PUBLIC GOOD

Be good to people, but don't ask for thanks.

When it rains in one land, let the other land rejoice.

P

PUNISHMENT

God does not throw stones.
[God punishes in other ways.]

Punishment rights no wrong,
but it deters a hundred
others.

If not inspired by its breast-
feeding,
no stick will ever right a child.
[It is a popular belief that a mother's breast-feeding of
her child will give it the personal character it holds for
the rest of its life.]

Killing deters killing.
— MUSAYLAMA THE LIAR (An 'impostor' prophet
contemporary to Prophet Muhammad who tried
to 'compete' with him.)

It is the duty of every one of the faithful to
listen to knowledge, to learn it by heart, to let
it be spread all over and to carry out public
good with it.
— HADITH

Let the clouds not shower on my fields,
If not sweeping the land far and wide;
We are all neighors in these wilds
Or out there at low ebb or high
tide.
— ABUL ALAA AL-MA'ARRI,
eleventh century poet

PUBLIC
PROPERTY

My mule together with the
abbey's will carry the load.
— IRAQI
[Abbeys in Iraq are mostly situated
in mountain areas, and are often
available for local public service.]

The bottom is mine and the ground is
the Sultan's.
['Sultan's land' alludes to common land.]

Q

The right answer at the right time is worth an orchard and its fruit.

QUARREL

Let us settle our account in the field rather than on the threshing-floor.

There was no intact wall between them.

Just like goats, they bleat from afar and butt when close.

The battle is heated, who can put out the flames?

It's a 'butchers' quarrel'.
– IRAQI
[In the Baghdad meat market, knives are first put aside.]

A hand banging its own cheeks.
[A domestic quarrel.]

QUERY

The query is a comedown, be it about the road.

A dog was asked how many stones were thrown at it each day. 'As many as there are thugs on the street,' it said.

A smile on her face, with venom in her teeth.

(Here come) Frowning countenances and deceitful hearts!

He slays with a needle.

If you meet with a villain burning in fire, add some more firewood.

The paths of villains are blocked by villains of their ilk.

'Whether you go to prison or you run away,' said the judge to the convict, 'I have branded you a rascal, anyway.'

REASON

Angels are ruled by reason, devils by passion, and man by both. Hence, he can make a choice between good and evil and he will be accountable for it.
– HADITH

You who strive in search of one,
There is but one upright Imam:
That is unfailingly our Reason,
Calling constantly from within.
– ABUL ALAA AL-MA'ARRI, eleventh century poet

Reason keeps one within one's limits, passion takes one beyond them. Only through reason can one achieve anything reasonable.
– Lilminber

RASCALS

You can't walk in front of him nor behind him.

He killed a man and walked behind his coffin.

There are no rogues like 'the godly ones'!
[Of some clergy.]

Make it up with a rascal, lest you descend to his ditch.
'I have cheated you, don't you know?'
'Then I have known you, can't you see?'
– PERSIAN

You know, my friends, with what a
brave carouse
I made a second marriage in my house?
Divorced barren Reason from my bed,
And took the daughter of vine as spouse.
– OMAR KHAYYAM (1048-1131), Persian
mathematician, astronomer and poet.

RECIPROCITY

Serve me a lunch, I'll serve you a dinner.

Give me fire and I'll give you the pot.

You scratch my back, I scratch yours.

Like a nephew and his aunt: he hopes she will
make him rich, and she is glad he tends her
sheep for free.
– TUNISIAN
Everything

(given) is a debt, even the tears of an eye.
[If someone 'wept' for you – that is, if they had cared
for you or had helped you at some point – you should
'weep' for them, when your help is required.]

Tit-for-tat, yet the one who started it was the
culprit.

He who gives a slap will receive its brother.

As you see me, I see you, O pretty one!

A sparrow at the pond: it laughs and people
laugh with it.

Today it is my burden, tomorrow it will be
yours.

'How many melons the camel broke!'
'And how many camels the melons did
break!'

She who gives you vinegar, give her
garlic.

He who sifts people, people will
winnow him.

If you keep taking from the
mountain and giving it
nothing, it will fall down.

Take and give, live and let
live.

REFUGE

Some flee from the flood into
the holocaust.

Only the more bitter will lead to the
bitter thing.

R

Lo! As for those whom the angels take (in death) while they wrong themselves, the angels will ask: What were you doing with your life? They will say: We were oppressed in the land. The angels will then say: Was not God's earth spacious enough for you that you fly for refuge?
– THE QUR'AN

RELATIONSHIP

Set out your tents apart and set your hearts together.
– HADITH

Only the bark is compassionate with the trunk.

To the one you do a good turn you are a prince; to the one you can do without you are an equal; and to whosoever you need you are in bondage.

My grandmother and your grandmother once span under the fig tree together.
[Of a remote relationship.]

RELATIVES

Father looks after son, son looks for his father's will.

The 'cockroach' writes down in the day and reads out at night.
[The daughter-in-law listens to her mother-in-law during the day and incites her husband at night.]

February sun be for my daughter-in-law, March sun be for my sister, and April sun be for me and for my household.
– LEVANTINE
[The mother-in-law allocates sun 'shares', setting aside the best for herself.]

Have a nephew made of clay and cut off his head in front of your boy.
[Children are jealous of relatives of their own age.]

The dog is the fox's cousin, yet they aren't too friendly.

Happy is the one who came out of the wall!
[That is, the one who has no relatives.]

R

When my mother-in-law fell in the river it was a mishap, and it was a tragedy that she came out safely.

The reckless son is a wart on the face of his father.
– AFGHAN

He whose wealth is gone, indifference will be his lot from kith and kin.

I wish you well and I wish you away.

When the Angel of Death appears, who won't direct him to their cousin?

For a thing you don't need, ask your stepfather.

An old friend is better than a new brother.

My brother and I are against our cousin; my cousin and I are against the alien.

Kiss your mother-in-law's hand before you kiss your wife.

He whose mother is a baker won't go hungry.

A brother is a brother, but you can buy a goat in the market-place.
– AFGHAN

Go back to your kith and kin, lest you perish from without and within.

A dog won't bite its brother.

Would that all my enemies were my kinsfolk, and that the land were full of them.

She who digs a pit for her sister will fall into it.

A husband is there and a child is born, but a brother once gone will never return.

A fool's business is with their own kinsfolk.

R

RELIGION

A person without fervor is a person without religion.
– LEVANTINE

The true faithful are those from whose hands and tongues people remain safe.
– HADITH

(O Muhammad, tell them:) There shall be no compulsion in religion; you have your religion and I have mine.
– THE QUR'AN

REPENTANCE

Sleep with sorrow, not with repentance.

More bitter than the colocynth is to repent too late.
[The colocynth is a small gourd-like fruit also known as the 'bitter apple'.]

The blow falls hard, but repentance comes harder.

What remains of life is not worthy of repentance.
[A proverb for an adamant sinner.]

Like your garments, you ought to wash your heart too.

It is good to roll in butter with strangers, and it's all right to taste a bitter cup with relatives.
– UZBEK

If truth and faith sway not thy
                    kinsman's breast,
To break off kinship with him were best.
– SHEIKH SADI, thirteenth century Persian Sufi poet

By penitence you may
                    exempt be
From wrath divine:
people's tongues you
                    can't flee.
– SHEIKH SADI,
thirteenth century
Persian Sufi poet

138

And then and then came Spring,
Rose-in-hand,
And my threadbare Penitence apieces tore;
Come, fill the Cup, and in the Fire of Spring
The Winter garment of Repentance fling!
– OMAR KHAYYAM (1048 - 1131), Persian mathematician, astronomer and poet

REPROACH

(Friendly) Reproach is the soap of hearts.

Reprove someone as much as you like them.

The one to be hanged was told to cover his legs decently. 'I'll remember that the next time,' he replied.

Lo! children of the times, hasten
to no judgment,
Should you hear reproaches from me;
I am but one of you to start with:
A mad race in a straying boat – out at sea!
– ABUL ALAA AL-MA'ARRI, eleventh century poet

RESPONSIBILITY

He who tied it with his hand shall untie it with his teeth.

Each one of you is a shepherd and each one of you is responsible for your dependents.
– HADITH

REST

Rest before you are exhausted, and rise before you fall asleep.

You can think best when at rest.

REVENGE

Blood washes away blood.

A Bedouin took revenge after forty years. It was said he was in a hurry.

R

If a man has sworn vengeance on you, you may go to sleep; if a woman, keep a guard throughout the night.

Kill and you will be killed, and your killer will be killed.

Revenge is the law of the lawless.
– Lilminber

REWARD

No one strikes iron for nothing.

Take him by the hand today, he will take you by the foot tomorrow.
[The ungrateful one.]

The mine is always bigger than the gem.
Give a laborer his fees before his sweat is dry.
– HADITH

Newly RICH

'How long have you been in this palace?'
'Arrived yesterday afternoon.'

O my bottom! Don't walk behind me!
– From ancient Aleppo
[The nouveau riche person wishes he or she could parade a portly posterior 'walking' in front of them.]

She was made known, and she was made rich.

The RICH

Those who enter hell's door will knock on it with a hammer of gold.

Three types of people are deplorable: the ignorant old, the extravagant poor, the lying rich.

The rich are affluent because the poor are deprived.
– IMAM ALI, seventh century, the fourth Khalif of Islam

There is no treasure without a demon (covetous of it).

R

The rich receive homage, the poor howls.

The rich person crosses the mountain in a coach, the poor person strays in the straight pathway.

If the rich man falls, it is an accident; if the poor man falls, he is 'drunken'.

A poor man saying a rat had eaten his cheese was a liar; a rich man telling of a rat swallowing his mule uttered the truth.

If a rich woman ate a snake, people would say it must have been tasty, if a poor woman ate it, they'd say she was crazy.

The poor person who gives a little only gives of her heart, and the rich person who gives much only gives of her pocket.

Someone earning their riches by toil and frugality? Do you know of any?

Prosperity is a bride whose home is modesty and whose gown is thankfulness of deeds, not of words.
– IMAM AS-SADIQ, ninth century scholar

The world does not give a lift in its coach but for a high fare.

If you give to a rich person, it is as if you throw into the sea.

The rich person sustains the fear of becoming poor, but the poor person enjoys the hope of becoming rich.

The wealthier they are, the more is their need.
[BUT: Little can suffice, much doesn't.]

The rich owe the thieves much, too much.
– TURKISH

A rich man enjoys the beauty of the world as much as a drunken man does the charm of a beauty.
– PERSIAN

God sent sacks to the rich, and bottoms to the poor.
['Sacks' of wealth and 'bottoms' of children.]

141

R

Some carry money and others are rich.
– Lilminber

RIGHT

Do things right to undo things done wrongly.

Nothing is right but the right thing.

What makes a thing right is not blatant might.

How many a wrong was committed in the name of the right!

He did the right thing in the wrong way; to do the wrong in the right way is the Devil's business.

Rather be wrong with everyone than be lonely in the right.

RIGHTS

If a person is out of sight, unguarded is their right.

Prove your right until some day you can recover it.

No right will be lost to her who searches for it.

Give me my due (right), yours is no problem.
– PERSIAN

Take and ask for more.
[OR: Take (even) a stone from a bad debtor.]

A tribe without rogues will lose its rights.
– Lilminber

The Almighty's beloved ones are the rich who have the humility of the poor, and the poor who have the magnanimity of the rich.
– SHEIKH SADI, thirteenth century Persian Sufi poet

If you have a loaf of bread and yet think there is in the world someone richer than you, you are then a fool.
– SHEIKH SADI

Tell the truth and give away your surplus.
– HADITH

Renowned as rich is better than renowned as poor.

Contentment is the undrainable source of riches.

If you are told : 'It's better to be poor' don't believe it.

ROOM

One rope, one acrobat.

The lane is narrow, and the mule is kicking up its heels.

A narrow place is big enough for a thousand friends; the whole world is not large enough for two enemies.

Take your things away, for I want to lay my things down!

ROSE

One rose can't make a springtime.

A rose begins to pale, yet it wafts its odor.

A rose can't nourish us, but it can please our soul.

The weeds are watered – thanks to the rose bushes.

Unable to find a blemish in a rose, someone called it 'O, bloody-cheeked one!'

RUDENESS

When the bear stood up to dance, he devoured seven souls.
['Bear' here alludes to a rough, brutal person.]

Grin in fury and people will run out of your way.

When gravel is thrown at it, move your head aside.
– PERSIAN

RULER

God save us from rulers and physicians.
[Their slips are fatal.]

A ruler's son is an orphan.
['Ruler's son' here implies the ruler's friend or follower; like an orphan, these would be left on their own when the patron is gone.]

If a ruler is just, the soldiers will be just too.

It would be curious if the Sultan was in the right, for he is ever flattered for whatever he says or does.

Would that the honor of the 'great' be great.

If you take your meals at the Sultan's you will have to strike with his sword.

Let a saint be deceased rather than a tyrant rise and rule.

In contrast with the pen, the sword is to rule,
As commands of its tongue will be missed
                    by no fool.
– AL-MUTANABI, tenth century poet

Better to rule devils than to be ruled by angels.

Nothing can feed you better than your own field, no one can rule you worse than your landlord.

If the monkey reigns, dance for it.
– EGYPTIAN

Wherever the turban turns, heads will turn with it.
– LIBYA
[Referring to the turbaned head of the ruler.]

One fallacy in the Sultan's head will hide a thousand truths.

When the ruler is a tyrant, the judge will be his hangman.

The ruler sleeps on an ant hill.
– AFGHAN

The minaret fell down, the ruler took the barber as a suspect.

She who is not happy with Moses's rule, she should be happy with Pharaoh's.

R

Don't trust the prince if his minister is not pleased with you.

The Pharaoh was asked what made him a tyrant. 'No one stood in my way,' he replied.
– In ancient Egypt

A thief who has not been caught is a king.

Think, in this batter'd Caravanserai,
Whose Portals are alternate Night and Day,
How Sultan after Sultan with his Pomp
Abode an Hour or Two, and went his way.
– OMAR KAHYYAM (1048 - 1131), Persian
mathematician, astronomer and poet

Bad rulers are cultivated by a state of unawareness among the ruled. Good rulers are only created by the well-meaning vigilance of the citizens of the land.
– Lilminber

Two persons are the foes of the state and faith: a king without clemency, and a clergyman with little learning.
– SHEIKH SADI, thirteenth century Persian Sufi poet

His daughter's baton

A story goes that an ancient chieftain became old and lost his ability to make the right judgments for his people. However, he had a wise daughter whom he asked to smack the ground with a baton whenever she heard him utter an injustice. Hence the saying: 'A baton need not be smacked for him,' which implies that someone is wise enough not to need reminding of how to manage their office.

An owl's dowry

A folk tale tells of an owl from Basra who asked the hand of the daughter of a fellow owl in Mosul for her son. In line with custom, this latter owl asked for a dowry for her daughter which she wanted to consist of a hundred ruined towns. As the owl from Basra knew that the would-be bride was worth it, she had to bring herself to agree to this steep demand. However, she asked the owl from Mosul to wait until the recently arrived ruler of her native Basra had stayed on for a while, by which time she hoped she would be able to deliver the desired dowry in full.
(Owls are looked upon as bad omens in the Arabic world, because they usually dwell in ruins. Basra and Mosul are the two biggest cities of Iraq after Baghdad, the capital.)

Qaraqoosh's rule

An Iraqi folk tale speaks of Qaraqoosh ('the black crow') who was a ruler famous for his curious verdicts. One of them concerned a thief who tried to break into a house through the window but fell down and broke his leg. He went to Qaraqoosh to complain against the household. Qaraqoosh ordered the house owner to be

cont'd

Sultan Qaraqoosh, who finally gave an order that a short man be brought to the spot and be hanged in execution of Qaraqooshian justice.

A time will come upon you when your chieftains will indulge in corrupting people and abandon their prayers. Those of you who will be ruled by them shall not serve under them as counsels, guards, tax collectors or storekeepers.
– HADITH

RUMORS

Rumors last seven days, news takes its time.

The rumor has put on its broken clog, traveled round the seven seas and come back home lame.

A rumor is what you didn't see but you just heard.

When everybody tells you 'You are an ass', thank God and bray.

hanged for the injury done to the thief. The owner claimed in defense that it was the carpenter who had not fixed the window properly. Qaraqoosh thought for a moment and ordered the arrest and hanging of the carpenter. The carpenter in turn said that it was the painter who was the culprit, because while he was working on the window, the painter's daughter had passed by and affected him with her charm, and in that way his attention was distracted and the work was faulty. Qaraqoosh had again to order the hanging of the painter. When the hangman proceeded, he found out that his house door was too low for the painter's long legs. As a result the painter's feet remained firmly on the threshold. This problem had to be raised once more to His Excellency,

S

If you fled from a tiger, don't chase it again.

Don't stir what is lying still; don't stop what is moving.

Close the door from which comes the wind.

He is like a locust: his legs don't belong to him.
[When caught, a locust saves itself by detaching its body from its legs leaving them with the holder.]

Take the paved way, be it long; dwell in the city even under a tyrant, and wed the faithful one be she an old maid.

Run away whilst your eyes
      are dry,
Before you're trapped
      and made to cry.

SAVING

We are destined to die, let us spend; we will live long, let us save.
– SUMERIAN

SAFETY

I don't want my blood to be poured in a golden tray.

Upon the sea it's true is boundless gain;
For thine safety upon the shore do remain.
– SHEIKH SADI, thirteenth century Persian Sufi poet

Watch the place where you think you are safe.
The jar can't always move to and fro in safety.
[Be careful in handling delicate matters.]

Each penny takes a chain to tie down.
– In ancient Aleppo, a Syrian city whose inhabitants had a reputation for frugality

To empty a jar is not like filling it up.

We saved them grain by grain; the camel came and scoffed them in one lump.
[The camel here alludes to a wasteful spendthrift.]

He who saves can do more than he who earns.

S

No chicken tomorrow for an egg today.

Childhood mates and life-savings are dear to the heart.

A white piaster will be good for a black day.

The SEA

The sea took two-thirds of the world, yet it claims the rest.

The sea is treacherous: they who escape it are newly born.
[Ancient Arabs avoided the sea.]

Come and live by the sea, or go and live away from it.
– LEVANTINE

You who crossed the sea, you had only changed your sky.
– PERSIAN

SEASONS

Had summertime parents, they would bid it farewell with tears.
– LEVANTINE

Summertime is a guest, winter is the host.
– LEVANTINE

Summer's mat is large.
[In summertime, one is free to move around freely and sit and enjoy oneself anywhere.]

Better than wool and leather, a person's skin is for all weather.

SECRETS

Dig deep and cover thickly.

Don't talk with a wall behind you.
– PERSIAN

What remains a secret is what never was.

Give your counsel to a thousand, but your secret to no one.

Your secret is your blood: don't let it flow but in your own veins.
[OR: Water once poured is never collected again.]

Your secret is your prisoner, once you let it slip out you will be its prisoner.

A secret is a sparrow: it takes wing once it leaves your hand.

Shared secrets are public news.

If you want to announce a secret, keep it in a woman's bosom.

S

He hangs his secrets on a minaret.

Asked why it did not speak up, the frog responded: 'Can one speak whose mouth is full of water?'

Fresh secrets are a mystery, old ones are history.
– Lilminber

Homes are full of secrets.

Don't listen to a secret and don't tell one.

Don't walk naked in the market place!
[Don't disclose your secret.]

She conceived in secret and was delivered in public.

Tell your secret to your friend and your friend will tell it to his.
– TURKISH

A Bedouin to whom a secret was confided was asked to be careful with it. 'I already forgot it,' he said.

SEEING

There are eyes in hearts.

The eyes are the spoon of speech.
[That is, they can 'measure' speech.]

See and stay!
[Explore the place, first!]

The first glance is not yours.
[Have another look!]

S

The eyes are the Devil's traps.
[Seeing is temptation.]

Fools speak of what they hear, the wise of what they see.

Lay aside what you hear and believe not all you see.
– BEDOUIN

SELF-INTEREST

A dog does not cry if hit by a bone.

A dog barking for you, rather than a dog barking against you.

Every prophet prays for his own people.

All songs known to bears are about peaches.
– TURKISH

Enlightened self-interest would see public prosperity as its own.
– Lilminber

They are brothers, but their pockets are not.

Everyone brings the fire closer to their own loaf.

No one calls their own oil turbid.
– LEVANTINE

SELFISHNESS

When you start to say 'Me!' you will start to worry.

Move your things away for I want to lay down mine.

He who eats alone will choke alone.

Self-lovers are hated by others.

SELF-JUDGMENT

Check upon yourself as if you were your own foe.

The highest virtue is to sit in judgment of your own self.

Consider your behavior when the door is not opened to your knocking.
– PERSIAN

Shall the one whose nose smells cut it off?
– TURKISH

The prophets are three and they were all sent to us!
[Implying that God sent Moses, Jesus and Muhammad to attempt to put right the shortcomings of human beings in vain. Usually said to reproach a member of one's own community or in remorse over an unwise act.]

150

SELF-RELIANCE

Rather eat sand than hold out your hand.

Nothing can scratch your back like your own fingernails.

Serve yourself rather than say 'Sire!' to a servant.

Only the tent pitched by your own hands will keep standing.

The illness is mine and God is my doctor.
[Accepting one's destiny.]

God created us and left us to ourselves.

Everyone is to drink from their own roof.
– LEVANTINE
[That is, from the well in the courtyard filled from the roof during the rainy season.]

You must take out your thorn with your own fingers.

Burn with your hair, but don't ask your aunt for fire.

Wipe your tears with your own hands.

Acre won't be bothered by the roar of the sea.
[Acre, an ancient port city in Palestine, was strongly walled and resisted invasions.]

A spider builds its home out of its own belly.

Rather tread your own loom than a prince's door.

SERVICE & SERVITUDE

The rose breeder is a servant of the thorn.
– TURKISH

Keep a mule, not a servant, for a long time.

She was asked why she swung her hips as she walked. 'I am the servant of the élite,' she said.

The new servant is faster than a gazelle.
– PERSIAN

The donkey is carrying on, why goad it then?

S

He who served me and received his fees is neither my master nor my slave.

The bell calls people to church, and it stays outside.
– LEVANTINE

I serve my lord and my lord serves his.

A slave is missing his servant and a servant, his assistant.

Service is not servitude and being served is not lordship; but serving one's own lust is the greatest slavery.
– SHEIKH SADI, thirteenth century Persian Sufi poet

Service is not a favor, but a favor is service.
– Lilminber

SETTLEMENT

Give me my right; yours is no problem!
– PERSIAN

Fix your right by good offices rather than with the kadi (judge).

No problem is ever settled until it is settled aright.

SHAME

It is shameful to meddle with shameful things.

If you meet with a shameless person be ashamed for them yourself.

'Lend me your face to quarrel with, please!'
[An 'appeal' to a brazen person.]

He is not a man who is not ashamed in front of men.

He has neither shame, nor sweat: he is shameless at home, he is shameless in the street.

The insolent one has wounds.
– TURKISH
[They goad the person's impudence.]

Gray hair does not shame, but shame may make gray hair.

SHARING

A shared pot never boils.

Don't wear two shirts while your uncle goes naked.

If you eat with a blind person, leave her some.

Sharing carries blessing.

S

A band of blind people walking with one stick.
[Inadequate sharing.]

'If you want a hare, here's one; if you want a gazelle, here's a hare,' said the lion to the wolf when they were hunting partners.
[On the sort of sharing between unequal partners.]

Take a share and give a share, and in it be fair.
– Lilminber

SHOWING-OFF

One ounce of boasting takes away a pound of virtue.
– SHEIKH SADI, thirteenth century Persian Sufi poet

The noise of an empty drum goes far and wide.
[OR: Like a drum, he is blown-up but empty inside.]

A naked woman with heavy make-up.
['Naked' here implies deprived and poor.]

SHYNESS

The blush is the color of chastity.

He who is shy before his cousin won't beget a child from her.
[Cousins are allowed to marry, but it is expressly of the 'Undesirable' category in the Islamic faith. The proverb suggests taking the initiative without shyness.]

SIGHING

Were sighing a remedy, I would have been healed already.

SIGNS

A good Spring ushers in a good year.

Were it not for its tongue, a sparrow would not be seen anywhere.

Throw clay onto the wall: if it doesn't stick, it will leave a mark anyway.

Fire leaves ashes behind.

The crooked line is the trail of the big ox.
['Big ox' here alludes to the person 'in charge' of a corrupt or failing enterprise.]

Things at the threshold show the nature of things inside.

It is not because the cock crows that the dawn breaks.

SILENCE

Silence is the wisdom of the few.

Silence is the most eloquent expression.

Silence is a response.

You can more easily make amends for your silence than for your speech.

If speech is of silver, silence is golden.

When invited to talk, silence is rebuke.

She who talks sows, she who listens reaps.

The fruit of silence is tranquility.

Talk to a friend, argue with a rival, and keep silent in a crowd.

A tannoor gets fire through its mouth.
[A tannoor is an open-mouthed clay oven. As fuel is thrown in through the 'mouth', this proverb is a counsel for silence.]

Someone passed by a man trying to instruct his donkey to talk, and told him: 'Your ass must be wiser than you are: it does not see any use in instructing you to be silent.'
– PERSIAN

Silence is prudent: it covers both secrets and blemishes.

They brought forth a daughter and called her Silence.

Silence is the big brother of the aphorism.
– PERSIAN

None preaches better than the ant, and it says nothing.

When silent, none can meddle with you:
Once you speak you must prove it's true.
– SHEIKH SADI, thirteenth century Persian Sufi poet

SIMILARITY

At the grain mill, we are all canaries.
[The roar overcomes individual voices.]

Only a crow looks like his father.

O, ye who are like us, come to us!

White dogs, black dogs – all are born of bitches.

At night all men are black.
[This is refers to the traditional flowing overdress worn by men which is mostly in black or gray; hence all men look alike at night.]

People are more different than similar and more similar than different – depending on which way one looks at it.
– Lilminber

O, sinner! Don't wait until you repent!

Tell the killer that he will be killed and the adulterer that he will die in poverty.

Nakedness comes from God, sin from the Devil.
[Nakedness here denotes innocence.]

Sin against God, and God will forgive you; sin against your fellow and God won't forgive you.
[It would then be up to the wronged person themselves to grant forgiveness.]

The sin is as big as the sinner.

The nearest to the heart is that which is forbidden.

Eschew sin, rather than ask for forgiveness.

The market of debauchery is always open.

To blaspheme at the impious is a sin unnoticed.

God's condescension and his mercy see
His servant's sins, and ashamed is he!
– SHEIKH SADI, thirteenth century Persian Sufi poet

SINGING

When the stomach is full it says to the head: Sing songs.

The canary is imprisoned because of its voice.

He drown'd my Honor in a shallow Cup,
And sold my Reputation for a Song.
– OMAR KHAYYAM (1048-1131), Persian mathematician, astronomer and poet.

The Prophet once passed by some feasting people, joined them, gave them a present and said: The good voice comes from Paradise.
– HADITH

SLEEP

He sleeps with hens and wakes up with cocks.
[The Arabic variant of 'Early to bed, early to rise', yet not without a hint of humor.]

Sleep is the Sultan.
[Sleep is powerful.]

God gives sleep to the bad in order that the good may rest undisturbed.
– SHEIKH SADI, thirteenth century Persian Sufi poet

People sleep well on a clear conscience.

How short is the night for those who sleep well.

Sleep won't come to the cold, the hungry or the fearful.

SOLITUDE

Eat alone and cough alone.

Solitude is the nest of thoughts.
– KURDISH

Be alone but not lonely.

SORROW

All things, save sorrow, start small and grow big.

A broken heart can be mended by a broken heart.

Surfeited pleasure leads to sorrow.

The eye of sorrow is narrow.

Water, greenery and a cheerful face will gladden the sad heart.

Sorrow is a good teacher.

Tears bear sorrow more lightly.

Happiness is a dream, sorrow is knowledge.
– PERSIAN

He asked her for a drink, she offered her tears.

Work is their bread, a little joy is their condiment, and sorrow is their daily wisdom – most people on this earth.
– Lilminber

SPEECH

The mouth is small, but it can ruin big houses.

A slip of the foot is a wound that can be healed; a slip of tongue is an injury that cannot.

S

In much talking, much thinking is half murdered.
– KAHLIL GIBRAN (1883-1931), Lebanese mystical writer, poet and artist

Strain your body, not your tongue.

Arguments would be few if people were honest in their speech.

Bad talk is the wind-breaking of the mouth.

Your tongue is your horse: if you guard it, it will guard you.

The tongue has no bone, yet it can wound.
– TURKISH

They who do not weigh their words will receive an answer to vex them.
– SHEIKH SADI, thirteenth century Persian Sufi poet

The more mature the mind, the less talk in the mouth.

Your tongue is your messenger, don't let it misrepresent you.

She who guards her tongue will save her head.

I wish I had a camel's neck; I would then taste words long before letting them out.
– HADITH

Your speech may be attractive, just and sweet,
Worthy to be approved by judgment nice;
But when once spoken, never the same
       repeat,
For once to swallow sweetness will suffice.
– SHEIKH SADI, thirteenth century Persian Sufi poet

Sweet talk can charm a snake out of its hole.

Proverbs are rivets of speech.
[They nail it down and hold it together.]

The best speech is a word of righteousness said at an oppressor's court.
– HADITH

He had a tongue that cut iron.

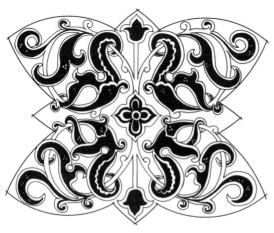

Thirty-two teeth do not clash in vain.
– PERSIAN

Some talk flows like a stream, some grinds like a mill and some flies like a bird.

A person can cover with their tongue what they keep in their heart.

Hold your tongue, but on four occasions: a truth to be uttered, a fallacy to be disproved, a favor to be thanked, and counsel to be given.
– HADITH

SPENDING

Bother your pocket, not your limbs.
[A proverb urging spending.]

Spend for you are living today, save for you will live tomorrow.

Wise spending makes up for half one's livelihood.

Spend today what is in your pocket, your lot of tomorrow will come with it.

SPONGERS

The age comes down from Heaven and the repast from next door.

She, who is used to your fare, salivates at the very sight of you.

A tray for Bahlool
Once Bahlool passed a man weaving a straw tray and asked him if he could make it a little larger.
    'Would you like to buy it, Bahlool?'
    'No, but perhaps someone will someday send me some provisions in it.'

A mouth to eat with, but no hand to work with.

Thanks to the roses that the thistles were watered.

What did you put of the capital to worry about the loss?

A loafer passed a company having a meal. He came and joined them at the table. When asked whether he knew any one of them, he pointed to the food and said: 'I know this!'

Listening takes more mind than speaking.

Ears weigh, eyes measure.

When the mind is overwhelmed words will fail.

He who says he doesn't like to talk, he doesn't like to listen either.

Sit awry but speak straight.

If you fear, don't speak; if you speak, don't fear.

Don't look into who said it, but into what was said.

Soft talk for a hard request.

When a person does not understand from a gesture, a long speech won't better them.

Talk of double-dealing sounds like honey, but works like venom.

S

START

Take heed and proceed.

If you start at counting sparrows, you won't sow the seeds.

Ride the donkey to take you to the camel.

Two-thirds of the way lies before the threshold.

If you don't send your basket down, none will fill it up for you.

He started a fire and then cried: 'O, God! Help!'

We've not yet spun, nor woven.
[We've hardly started...]

Don't start a job that you don't intend to finish.

The load was unbalanced right from the door of the tent.
[This refers to a badly loaded camel, with the result that the goods fall off midway – a bad start.]

The merit belongs to the one who did it first.

A push forward (is needed) for the start.

At long last he gave her a kiss.
[Apparently of a shy groom; the moral being that after long hesitation someone did at last make a start.]

Abilities start with a vision and end with achievements.
– Lilminber

STONE

No stone is left over on the road, which is good for a wall.

A stone that you belittle can wound you.

A rolling stone is no good as a stool.
– TURKISH

If your stone is too big, you can't throw it (at a target).

A stone not in your way need not bother you.

A stone of the road.
[A good-for-nothing person.]

Draw on water and pinch a stone!
[Of something that is futile.]

STORY

A passing cloud and its shadow, and a traveler and his stories.

A fable is a bridge which leads to a truth.

She was asked to tell a story; 'Joseph was lost and found!' she said.
[Of abridging a story too much. It relates here to the Qur'anic account of Prophet Joseph going astray in Egypt and being found thrown into a well, of how Pharaoh's amorous wife tried to seduce him, and of his resistance to temptation.]

STRANGER

O, stranger! Be humble and be gentle.

Don't ask a naked man where his clothes are, or a stranger where his home is.
– KAHLIL GIBRAN (1883-1931), Lebanese mystical writer, poet and artist.
[Just extend a helping hand if you can.]

S

A stranger is to spend his night at an inn, be he the Sultan.

A stranger is a comrade to a stranger.

Let a stranger show what she can do.

A stranger's funeral is lonesome.

The house is our father's; the stranger expelled us from it!
[ALSO: An alien hand destroys a thriving house.]

Rather in prison with a friend than in a garden with a stranger.

Away from home is an estrangement.

The poor are strangers at home, the rich are at home in a foreign land.

STRIKE

If you strike, strike hard; if you give food, make sated.

A strike for a strike could bring nearer to peace.

Shake up, but don't strike.

SUCCESS

When the dark-minded robber finds success,
What cares he for the caravan's distress?
– SHEIKH SADI, thirteenth century Persian Sufi poet

Success is never final, failure is never fatal. It's courage that counts.

No one can harvest glory on a bed of feathers.

Success is not the fruit of your ambition but of your desire to achieve.
– Lilminber

SUFFERING

Someone's cake is being baked on someone else's burning beard.

Suffering is the fountain of wisdom.
– SUFI

Suffering is the teacher of fools, reason is the teacher of the wise.
– SHEIKH SADI, thirteenth century Persian Sufi poet

SUSPICION

Under the aba (robe) there is something peculiar!

Don't enter the house of the suspicious, nor eat at the boaster's.

S

When you are in doubt, abstain.

He who puts his head into the bran, chickens will come and peck it for him.

Leave aside what you hear and do not believe all that you see.

She suspects her own garments.

Take all who enter your house as thieves, and your house will be safe.

SUSPENSE

Let me go lest I cry, hold me tight lest I fall.

He divorced her and kept clinging to her legs.

Hesitation cuts bluntly.

SWEET

No sweet without sweat.

Those who tasted sweetness are to taste bitterness as well.

If you find something sweeter than honey, go and lick it.

Sweets, sweets, I like sweets: fill my mouth with sweets, or else.. I'll leave it open!
[The blackmailer speaks.]

The serpent and the shepherd
A folk tale goes that a shepherd's son used to go to a snake living near a treasure. It gave him a piece of gold each day he went there. Out of greed, however, he tried to kill the snake and take the treasure for himself. He struck it with an ax and cut off its tail. The snake jumped at him, bit him and killed him. His father then came to the snake for reconciliation. 'Neither can I forget about my tail, nor can you about the tomb of your son,' said the snake in rejection of his placatory offer.

His wool is red!
[Suspicion invariably falls on him even when he is not guilty of anything wrong. OR: The lion stands suspicious, even if it spends the night in hunger.]

You got only wet firewood from me!
– PERSIAN

Eat things sweet and live with the sweet one, eat things bitter, but don't live with the bitter one.

162

T

As desert sand is tiresome to the traveler; so is un-ending chatter to the lover of silence.

TACT

Don't describe the beauty of rainbow to a blind person.
– PERSIAN

Don't call the one-eyed person 'One-eyed!'

The whiskers of the cat and a person's tact are indispensable.
[In order to maintain a balance.]

Learn tact from the tactless.

TALKATIVENESS

How nice if someone dines out of one's own plate and lends me their ears for a while!
[A chatterbox's way of hiring his audience's ears.]

Take a seat away and say whatsoever you may.

Apprentice your son to a barber and he will learn to be a talker.
– IRAQI
[Barbers in Iraq usually entertain their customers by talking to them while working on their heads.]

T

TASTE

Tastes are not to argue about.

Were it not for the diversity of taste, goods would get stale in the shops.

Filling a cup is not in good taste.
– LEVANTINE
[This is so in the Levant; but among Bedouin people in the countryside, the custom is to present water or drinks in a full glass or cup.]

TAX

One can have a lord, one can have a ruler, but the one to fear is the tax collector.
– SUMERIAN

A poor person's tax goes to the rich, and a rich person's tax goes from one of their pockets to the other.
– Lilminber

The zaka
In the Islamic world tithing one's earnings has a long tradition. 'Zaka' literally means 'purification' and is different from almsgiving. The argument for it goes that people are not always honest about the way they gain their incomes. And so, zaka is meant to be a sort of redemption of their gross earnings. This is over and above the revenues which are to be collected to regulate public services needed in a given time or community. The point here is that the faithful would not be inclined to cheat when having to meet this duty.

TEARS

Save your tears for the time of weeping.

A thousand weeping eyes would not be so sad as the eye with one tear from an old man.
– KAHLIL GIBRAN (1883 – 1931), Lebanese mystical writer, poet and artist

Tears are women's wealth.

A harlot's tears are dear and sincere.

If we shed tears for everyone we shall end up blind.

Everything is a debt, even the tears of the eye.

What tears express
Tears are the words of diverse emotions. They are the relief of sorrow and the expression of joy; they come out of disappointment or signal success. They are a weapon, they are defense. They admire and they thank. They are sweet and they soothe. They are the furthermost part of emotion. They are the daughter of righteousness. Yet they cannot relieve wrath, as wrath mostly demands action to put things right.
– Lilminber

TEMPTATION

He who touches honey will lick it off his finger.

Scattered grain attracts birds from Tunis to Taza.
– MOROCCAN

Devils tempt all, but the idle person tempts all devils.

How can the crow sleep when the figs are ripe?
– PERSIAN

Crime tempts the wicked.
– PERSIAN

May God shield us from the temptation of ourselves.
– From a prayer

Don't lead the young into temptation; let them handle it in their own time in their own way.
– Lilminber

TERROR

Terror has come, gone is the pain.

A blow from a terror-stricken one won't hurt.

When the hawk cries, little birds stop singing.

An outright death is better than to live lifelong in fear.

TEST

Gold is proven by the touchstone; the kadi (judge) is proven by gold.

Through testing a person emerges dignified or discredited.

The contents of the pot are revealed by the spoon.

THIEF

He got hungry and stole, and stole and got hungry.

Her hands are light, her hands are 'clean'.

The thief of the night sees with the eyes of the day.
[By exploring the place beforehand in daytime.]

If you want to strike, strike a prince; if you want to steal, steal silk.
[OR: If you want to steal, steal a province.]

T

If you are not a thief, why then is your hand is my pocket?
— PERSIAN

The sun will some day rise on the thieves!

Should I believe you or the rooster's tail
(showing from your pocket)?
— PERSIAN
[ALSO: There are feathers in your hair, O chicken thief! — PERSIAN]

Going out to steal, a thief raises his head in prayers: 'Open up, dear God!'

She steals kohl from the eye!

He who wants to steal a minaret must dig a well for it, first.

Stolen things move in the dark.

The fortune-teller collected what was left over by the thief.
— IRAQI
[Vicitims in ancient Baghdad used to go to fortune-tellers to help find thieves after a burglary.]

The robber dislodged the door and girded himself with the threshold!

The miser only lost either to the thief or to the heir.

The rich owe thieves much, too much.
— TURKISH

Cold teaches the stealing of bed-covers.

The clever thief won't steal from his own district.

He was asked whether he could steal and he

A strong thief asks the household: 'Come and help me out!'
— IRAQI
[This Iraqi saying was quoted by an American writer relating to the US war in Vietnam, and how the US used the Vietnamese against their own country.]

Suspicious is the thief, and it is the leper that scratches.

A thief in the middle of the night is on time.

The stolen oil was just as much as the thief needed.

Take the thief before he takes you.

The adulterer fears for his wife, and the thief for his house.

In his lifetime he was a thief, and in his death he became an informer.
[His death uncovered his accomplices.]

said yes; he was asked whether he could hide and he said no. 'Sorry, you aren't a thief, then' he was told.

A thief was asked to swear (in court). 'Here is my salvation,' he thought.
[He thought by swearing by his 'innocence' he could get away with it.]

You may complain, or cry, Alack!
The thieves won't give your gold back!
– SHEIKH SADI, thirteenth century Persian Sufi poet

Bahlool makes peace
A story goes that Bahlool was once in bed on a cold winter night when he heard some noise on the road. Wrapping his bed-cover around him, he went out to see what was going on and saw some people quarreling. As he approached to appease them, they grabbed the cover and ran away with it. When he returned to bed, his wife asked him what had happened. 'I made peace for the bed-cover,' he told her.

Bahlool moves house
Once a thief broke into Bahlool's house and carried his possessions away. Bahlool followed him to his place and when the thief got into his house, Bahlool entered after him. 'What are you doing here?' yelled the thief. 'I am the one whom you are moving to this house, sir,' said Bahlool.

Bahlool's compassion
As Bahlool was a poor man, a thief once broke into his house but found nothing to steal. Seeing that the thief left empty-handed, compassionate Bahlool went out himself and stole a carpet from a rich man and sent it to the thief, his fellow in poverty, in order to console him.

TIME

Time passes silently, greeting no one!

Time is a sword, if you don't 'cut' it, it will cut you.

T

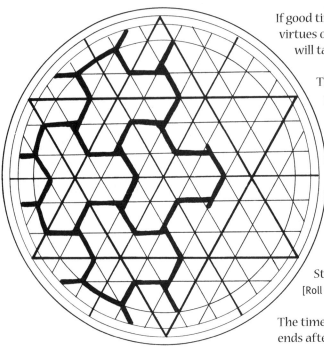

If good times favor you, they lend you the virtues of others; and if they dodge you, they will take yours away.

The remedy of ill times is to be patient with them.

Times sell and buyers lose.

The times are pregnant with black demons.

Take from your table what you please, and from the times what they please.

Stay a wheel if hard times roll over you.
[Roll with them.]

The times are our host, and their hospitality ends after three days

Honor the noble one whom the times had betrayed.
– HADITH

Time rides on the back of a horse.
[It passes too fast.]

The hasty and the tardy will both meet at the ferry.

The bird of time has but a little way
To flutter – and the bird is on the wing.
– OMAR KHAYYAM (1048 – 1131), Persian mathematician, astronomer and poet

The TIMES

Trust not the sea, trust not the times.
[Until the birth of Islam in the seventh century, ancient Arabs used to avoid the sea.]

If hard times press you, press your arm.
[Be more diligent.]

TIMING

Press clay while it is still wet, and plant the root when it's green.

Don't weep for a person man before they are dead.

Save a stick for the time of beating.

Actions without timing go astray like a gust of wind.

T

TOGETHERNESS

Two pieces of wood burn higher together.

If you leave me, you'll be alone; if I leave you I'll be lonely.

Birds of a kind are a cheerful company.

TOIL

Toil, then play.

Your comrade to the flourmill is the hardship of the mountain road.
– LEVANTINE

Not all who gained toiled, but all those that earned did.
– PERSIAN

Do you want pearls? Go, then, and plunge into the sea. Do you want a bride? Then fork out your silver.

Prosperity is the toil of man; extravagance is God's test of him.
– SHEIKH SADI, thirteenth century Persian Sufi poet

TOLERANCE

The larger vessel can contain the smaller one.

Tolerance is a big place for those of different minds to meet. Tolerance is understanding subdued with patience.
– Lilminber

Tolerance is generosity. Tolerance is a sign of faith.
– HADITH

TOMORROW

Pour wine today, friend of mine,
For tomorrow is another day.
– ABU NAWWAS, tenth century poet

Each tongue is a man.
[ALSO: To speak a people's tongue is safe-conduct amongst them.]

A person's tongue is their horse: if it trips up, they will fall down.

If your tongue is your spokesperson, don't let it misrepresent you.
– IMAM ALI, seventh century, the fourth Khalif of Islam

Tongue can show you up, tongue can cover you up.
– PERSIAN

Hold your tongue save in these occasions: to defend right, to denounce wrong, to thank a favour and to give counsel if asked for it.
– HADITH

Where 'Tomorrow' was planted, no plantation was found.

When tomorrow comes, think tomorrow's thoughts.

Ah, fill the Cups: what boots it to repeat,
How Time is slipping underneath our Feet,
Unborn tomorrow and dead yesterday,
Why fret about them if today is sweet.
– OMAR KHAYYAM (1048-1131), Syrian mystical writer, poet and artist

No soul knows what it will tomorrow gain, nor in which land it will expire.
– THE QUR'AN

He who despairs gives license to his tongue.
– SHEIKH SADI, thirteenth century Persian Sufi poet

Her fire is on the tip of her tongue.
[She is sharp-tongued.]

TOWN

Every village has a road to the town.

Praise all towns, but live in your own.

God creates people, and people build towns.
– PERSIAN

Build yourself a home in every town.
[Have friends everywhere.]

Should We determine to doom a town,
We would then allow its copious loose-living

TONGUE/LANGUAGE

Argue in Persian, reproach in Turkish, and flatter in Arabic.

élite to spread corruption in it.
– THE QUR'AN

TRAVEL

Travel is both school and picnic.

Live and see, move around and see more.

When you go away guard your head, when you come back guard your household.

Who did not wander did not know people.

A traveler without observation is a bird that has not left its nest.
– PERSIAN

Travel is a scale of character.
[Of old, travel was an enterprise of great discomfort which showed how much a traveler could bear through long journeys in a camel caravan or on horseback.]

When a traveler hears about dogs, he remembers about the stick.

A person earns merit when they die or when they travel.

You who entered Egypt, you would meet with many of your like.

He has been to Akka and Mecca!
[He has traveled far and wide. Akka here refers to Acre, a sea-port in Palestine.]

With a full moon you can't go far, but you can by a little twinkling star.

When you enter a town, swear by its gods.

A traveler has too many stories to tell.

One rider is a devil, two riders are two devils, and three riders are a traveling company.
– HADITH

Honor the traveler, even if he is an infidel.
– HADITH

The merits of travel

An ancient poem has it that travelers are blessed in five ways. They leave home worries behind, their knowledge of other peoples and foreign lands is enhanced, they will be entertained by new company, they travel trading and making gains, and when they return, they are dearly welcomed with feasting.

Sheikh Sadi and the traveler

Here is a story by Sheikh Sadi, a thirteenth century Persian mystic, about a boastful traveler.

I once met with a merchant who had a hundred and fifty camels of burden and forty slaves and servants. One night, on the Island of Kish, he took me to his room, and did not cease the whole night from talking in a vaunting fashion, and saying: "I have such a correspondent in Turkistan, and such an agency in Hindustan; and this paper is the title-deed of such a piece of ground, and for such a thing I have such a person as security." At one time he said: "I intend to go to Alexandria, as the climate is agreeable there." At another: "No! for the western sea is boisterous. O Sadi! I have one more journey before me: when that is accomplished I shall retire for the rest of my life and give up trading." I said: "What journey is that?" He replied: "I shall take Persian sulfur to China, for I have heard that it brings a prodigious price out there; and thence I shall take Chinaware to Greece, and Grecian brocade to India, and Indian steel to Aleppo, and mirrors of Aleppo to Yemen, and stripped cloth of Yemen to Persia, and after that I shall give trading up and sit at home in my shop." He continued for some time rambling in this strain until he had no power to utter more. Then he said. "O Sadi! do thou say something of what thou hast seen and heard." I replied: "Thou hast not left a single thing to talk about, Sir."

Sheikh Sadi then recited:

Hast thou not heard what once a
merchant cried,
As in the desert from his beast he sank?
The worldly one's greedy eye is satisfied
But by contentment or the graveyard
dank.

T

TREE

Good tree gives good fruit.

The tree that can't shade its roots is to be cut off from them.

There is nothing like a tree. It gives you fruit, you shake it and throw stones at it, and then you come and sit under its shade; yet it welcomes you keeping silent all the time.

Honor your aunt the date palm.
– HADITH
[Dates are provide good nourishment, which together with camel milk make the main daily means of sustenance for many desert Arabs.]

If Doomsday approaches whilst one of you has a sapling at hand, let them put Doomsday off if they can until they plunge the sapling into the soil.
– HADTIH

TRIFLE

There were screams and witnesses: on the scene was but a hedgehog.

A pail told the well: 'Take me, I am coming!' 'Many a poor thing like yourself comes down into my bottom everyday!' said the well.
[OR: A mosquito told a wall: 'Hold on, I am perching on your shoulder!']

Barking dogs won't bother the moon.

She has a palm-tree in Damascus, don't you know?
– IRAQI
[For people in Iraq, which has an abundance of palm trees, this is a trifle in far-away Damascus.]

A hundred sparrows won't fill up a pot.

Dew never filled a well.

The mountain labored and brought forth a mouse.
– PERSIAN

A straw showed upon the waves.

A minaret fell down in Istanbul, someone screamed in Aleppo.

When the horse was shod, the scarab beetle stretched out its feet.

If a piece of gravel is thrown at you, move your head aside.
– PERSIAN

TROUBLE

His beard is plucked out!
[He is in great trouble.]

Some can only live on trouble, others have to live with it.
– Lilminber

Don't let your bird fly in dusty air.

A passing summer cloud that will soon be gone.

TRUST

Hobble your camel and trust in God.

Put a stone on your lot and sleep on it.
[...if the trustworthy are no longer there.]

A person who makes mistakes inspires more trust than one who is ever sure of herself.

To put your trust in others takes more self-confidence than having it from them.
– Lilminber

'I do believe you, my Lord, yet I want my heart to rest at ease!'
– Prophet Abraham to God in THE QUR'AN

If trust is being lost, put your things under your armpit.

TRUTH

Who takes the course of truth will create life.
– SUMERIAN

The distance to truth is four fingers.
[That is, between the hearing ears and the seeing eyes.]

Truth may walk around unarmed through the world.

Truth said: 'Leave me naked, I have nothing to be ashamed of.'

The truth is half tears and half smiles.
– MALTESE

Truth, like roses, often blossoms upon a thorny stem.
– PERSIAN

If you speak the truth don't fix your tent close to mine!

T

Never tell the truth unless you are already in the saddle.
– TURKISH

When you launch the spear of truth, dip its point in honey.
– ANDALUSIAN

Soften your voice and harden your truth.

Take it from the drunkard's mouth, not from the sober one's.

Truth is but covered with a straw.
[..for those that search for it.]

Even from a crooked chimney the smoke emerges straight.
– TURKISH
[OR: A sack of sand can't stand upright. – TURKISH]

A wise man in search of truth is like the one who lost a pearl in the sand; he must collect lumps, and then sift them all until he recovers the little, brilliant pearl.
– IMAM ALI, seventh century, the fourth Khalif of Islam

The righteous one is the one who speaks the truth, not the one who speaks first.

Rather a neat lie than a sloppy truth.

Truth is like a sponge: it won't sink.

Both truth and the sword engage naked in battle.

If I utter fallacies amongst men,
I may raise my voice ever high;
But if I say the naked truth,
I may only whisper with a sigh.
– ABUL ALAA AL-MA'ARRI, eleventh century poet

If with a lie you want to play safe, it will be safer to play with truth.

Half a truth is a complete fallacy.

Lay it bare to them, do not keep it covered.
– THE QUR'AN

TYRANNY

Who would say that the lion's mouth stinks?

He pulled down a town and built himself a castle.
[OR: He burns a city to light a fireplace.]

The Pharaoh made his people poor and made them obedient.

When the ruler is a tyrant, the kadi (judge) will become his hangman.

The Pharaoh was asked what made him a tyrant. 'No one stood in my way,' he replied.

The kadi's servant died and had a huge funeral; the kadi died and no one walked behind his coffin.

Has anyone ever heard of the one who had to look for a dentist in another country, because he could not open his mouth in his own?
– LEVANTINE

Rather a hundred years of tyranny than one night of sedition.

If the lion does not like funerals, the fox need not die.

The Devil is cursed in his presence, the Sultan in his absence.

Let them be glad who reach Doomsday together with a tyrant.
[The angels would then be too busy reckoning the long account of the monstrous sinner to bother about smaller fry.]

That unity which has not its origin in the multitude is but tyranny.
– ABDUL QASIM, Egyptian writer

Kiss the hand, which you can't cut off.

U

It is one thing to read, it is another to comprehend.

Moving rocks is easier than making him understand who does not want to.
– IMAM ALI, seventh century, the fourth Khalif of Islam

To understand someone is to have sympathy for them.

UNITY

A bundle of sticks is harder to break.
[Strength in unity.]

A hand is but finger and finger staying together.

Those united will grind the mountain to powder.
– UZBEK

That unity which has not its origin in the multitude is but tyranny.
– ABDUL QASIM, contemporary Egyptian writer

UNDERSTANDING

She who can't understand a people is not one of them.

Explain to the crazy one, and he will understand; explain to a fool and he won't.

He who won't understand from a wink, talk to him with a stick.

Clear intentions make understanding easy.
– Lilminber

UNIVERSE & FAITH

It's nothing but a magic Shadow-show,
Play'd in a Box whose Candle is the Sun,
Round which we Phantom Figures come and go,
Not knowing whose game it is, or whose fun.
– OMAR KHAYYAM (1048-1131), Persian mathematician, astronomer and poet

U

Thou thinkst Thou art but tiny and trivial,
Yet within Thee dwells the whole Universe!
In Thee lie Creation secrets of the Immortal,
To Whom we all turn for better or for worse.
– IMAM ALI, seventh century, fourth Khalif of Islam

Or do you think Man is created in vain?
– THE QUR'AN

Unto God belong the easts and the wests, and
whithersoever you turn your faces, there is
the face of God. God is Omnipresent and
Omniscient.
– THE QUR'AN

UNLIKELIHOOD

To expect leftover firewood from the fires
of Hell!
[OR: .. a bone from hungry dogs!]

A needle fell into the well: the deaf one heard
it falling and the blind one saw it going down.

An impotent man and a barren woman:
where has the child come from, then?
– ANDALUSIAN

The mean person's promise will come true
only when a rooster will an egg lay.

UNPREPAREDNESS

She was at the harvest with a broken sickle.

Our bows are in Persia and the arrows will
come soon!
– IRAQI
[Said ironically on being suddenly in a grave situation.]

He who rides a horse of wind with legs of wax
will melt in the sun.

UNWELCOME

A guest not invited may sit on the (straw)
mat.

Was it my camel and
myself who rendered the
'khan' so narrow?
– IRAQI
[A khan is a spacious inn, so
called in Iraq because traveling Khans of old often used
them. Yet the visitor and camel of the proverb are not
welcome there.]

The house is yours, but the mosque should be
warmer for you!

The soulless, stingy, dull and senseless wight,
Bids thee go, saying: 'There's no one in' – he's
right!
– SHEIKH SADI, thirteenth century Persian Sufi
poet

UPS & DOWNS

One time a rooster, another time a sparrow;
one time empty, another time glutted.
– SUMERIAN

Be not overjoyed, O bully bear; some day your
bottom will be beaten again by a stick.

One arrow is for you, another is against you.

USEFULNESS

Don't throw a stone into the well where you drink.

If you can't be a star in the heavens, be a candle on earth.
– PERSIAN

A handful of bees is more useful than a sack of flies.
– TURKISH

A hair from a pig's skin!
[...could also be useful! OR: Venom could also heal.]

Your skills are as good for us as the builder's to Bedouins.
[They are not useful to us.]

Useful intelligence
A story goes that a man wanted to test the intelligence of his two sons. So he gave them ten dirhams (coins) each and asked them to buy the cheapest thing that would fill up the house. One of them bought a full load of hay for ten dirhams and the other bought a candle for one dirham.

Bahlool's logic
Bahlool was once asked which was more useful, the sun or the moon. 'The moon, of course,' he said. 'How is that, Master Bahlool?' he was asked. 'Because the sun shines in daytime when people can already see, but the moon shines at night when it is dark,' he explained.

V

The barefooted threw himself onto the naked one (asking for help)!

He looked at an elephant and stabbed its shadow.

A nut in a toothless mouth.

His spout pours outwards.
– LEVANTINE
[This refers to rainwater which is made to pour from the roof into the yard leading to the household's well. Here the inference is that the person tends to favor people other than their own kinsfolk or friends.]

A mouse digs a hole and fills it up again.

She is cooking gravel.

Debate of the deaf.

He struggles with his own shadow.

Come on, let us fight and make friends again!

In VAIN

My fingers were burning; would that I was cooking something.

Don't launch an arrow at a statue of iron.

Much hobbling but little hunting.

Draw on water and pinch a stone.

She is blowing into a torn sack.

They pulled down a mosque and erected a minaret.

A man sold his son for need, another bought him on credit.

He chased the wind which felled his turban.
– KURDISH

A cry in a valley.

Slaughterhouse dogs have bloodstained mouths, yet they stay hungry.
[For they are not given meat to eat.]

A bug looking for a pair of shoes.

Of such broken needles we have heaps.

180

Don't strike cold iron!
[The Arabic variant of 'Strike when the iron is hot.']

After great effort, he 'explained': 'Water is water.'

Bahlool sold his half of the house and bought the other half.

If the camels are lost, count their halters.

What the camel had plowed, it leveled with its hooves.

Give me a lift home and I'll give you a lift back.

She threw stones at the eagles!

He pulled down a town and crowned himself on the ruins.

If it rained all year long, would the sea turn into sweet water?
– MALAYSIAN

'Your sling has no stone.'
'Yes, I know. But look, the bird is flying!'

The good in vain their rays will pour
On those whose hearts are bad at the core.
– SHEIKH SADI, thirteenth century Persian Sufi poet

VANITY

Vanity is a transparent gown.

There are still some unground grains in his head.

The length of the loaf may shorten the brain.
['Loaf' here alludes to one's fortunes.]

An owl's vanity
An owl was once asked why its head was so big; 'Because I am a chieftain,' it said. 'But why is your tail so short?' it was asked again. 'Because I am a little chick,' it responded.
   'From head to tail you lied twice, then,' it was told.
[Owls are looked upon as bad omens in the Arabic world, because they usually live around ruins.]

She thinks she is ten measures of wheat done up in a gaudy sack!

The roof of vanity is ignorance and the ceiling is conceit.
– Lilminber

The conceited think that the audience's ovation is the end of their career's striving.
– ABDUL WAHHAB, contemporary Egyptian entertainer

Vanity is the failure of wisdom.

Arrogance is consolation for those who are doomed to stay small.

An ounce of vanity spoils a hundredweight of merit.
– SHEIKH SADI, thirteenth century Persian Sufi poet

The arrogant one did meet with the rogue!
[They are only fit to fight each other.]

Here is my uncle, and there is my aunt – and to them I am somebody!

Now that the pumpkin is large and round, it has forgotten its origins.

There is a pair of scissors for every pair of mustaches.
[For cutting them down to size.]

The lofty have a rival in God.
[OR: God is bigger than the Sultan.]

And walk not on the earth arrogantly. Lo! You cannot rend the earth, nor can you stretch out to the height of the mountains.
– THE QUR'AN

VARIETY

A cloud and its shadow and a land and its fashions.
[...show the variety of life.]

If you have two loaves, sell one and buy yourself a rose.

The variety of the rainbow makes it appeal.
– TURKISH

The variety of small things is nicer than the uniformity of big things.
– PERSIAN

The VEIL

The veil covers shortcomings, exposure uncovers pockets.
– EGYPTIAN
[The suggestion here is that women who don't veil themselves pay the higher costs of maintaining their fashionable clothes.]

Behind the veil there are 'serpents'.
– In ancient Aleppo

The thicker the veil, the less worth lifting.
– TURKISH

She covered her face and uncovered her legs.

You may cut your skirt short, daughter, but who is going to look at it?
[A mother to her veiled daughter. The short skirt would indeed be invisible under the veil.]

The veil and Islam

From times of old, the veil has been used as a protection against sandstorms and a disguise in the lonely Arabian desert. Although Islam demands modesty of appearance from men and women alike, shari'ah (Islamic law) does not stipulate any veiling of the face. In fact it demands full uncovering of it, for instance in juridical places and in public, in order to establish personal identity. In the ancient Arabic world the practice of veiling is believed to have evolved from cosmopolitan rich élites and their 'harem' practice which is quite alien to native Arabic culture.

V

VICE

Vice is not learnt at school.

To contemplate sin is sin.

VIRTUE

Virtue pardons the wicked as the sandal-tree perfumes the ax which strikes it.
— SHEIKH SADI, thirteenth century Persian Sufi poet

You who would sum my virtue up, enough
                    you'll find
In outward semblance; yet to my secret
                    failings be blind.
— SHEIKH SADI

VOCATION

Either you like your vocation or you need it.

If you are good at it, it's a career; if not, it's noise.

The up-to-date seamstress – she lost the needle and found the thimble.
[Said of someone who is not that good at their chosen vocation.]

One would be spared half the effort should one choose one's father's career.

The one who can make a pin can make a needle.

A scholar was asked what a person's best virtue was. 'A name earned through a career,' he replied.

If you are a reaper, sharpen your sickle; if an ironsmith, blow your fire.

A fellow craftsman is your foe, even if he is your brother; a fellow craftsman is your brother, even if he is your foe.

The job doesn't dishonor the person, but the person may dishonor the job.

A career is a good caring mother.

A craft is a golden bracelet round your hand.

If you want to go to the flour mill you should not be bothered by the dust of the road.

V

His job is uncovered like the bottom of a goat.

A mule and a donkey are the sweetness of the muleteer.

Test the carpenter at the knot.

The person with two vocations masters neither.

The 'prosperous' shoe-repairer
The saying goes: The shoe-repairer did prosper in Ifach!

I was curious about this ironic saying. Ifach is an Iraqi village (situated near an ancient Sumerian site called Nupper along the Euphrates) whose inhabitants were said to wear no shoes; so 'prosper' here actually means 'went bankrupt'. When I visited Ifach, I was told by the person sitting next to me at a wayside café that the cause for the poor shoe-repairer's decline was because Ifachis 'wear no old shoes'. This was obviously not true – but then again I had not seen anyone not wearing shoes either. Whatever its origins, the moral of this saying is that one should offer one's services only where they are needed, otherwise one would likely meet with the kind of 'prosperity' that befell the hapless shoe-repairer in Ifach.

W

You go and take others' land, and they will come and take yours.
– SUMERIAN

The old think of dying, the young of wandering.

WAR

Arms are present and reason is absent.

They who know it not will welcome it with a dance!
– IRAQI

They who gained a land without war may give it away without loss.
[It also implies 'Easily gained, quickly lost.' OR: They who entered the land without making war could leave it in peace.]

I see your heart's with me and your sword's against me! Take my head, then, but not my hand!
– IMAM HUSSAIN, the Prophet's grandson, the Prince of Martyrs, to those who slew him and his family in Kerbela, eighth century.

WANDERING

Travel teaches, wandering is for fools.
– PERSIAN

Don't ask a vagabond his route, nor inquire about his means.

If you don't wander, you won't know people.

From land to land I lost my children, from house to house, I lost my belongings.
– Lilminber

Only those who are afraid to be called cowards will go to war.

And it may happen that a war is provoked by a word.

W

Bahlool in the battlefield

A folk tale of yore goes that Bahlool was once asked to join a battle against the enemies of the king of his time. In vain he pleaded to be excused, because he was not good at fighting and feared a sticky end. But as the king wished to amuse himself by seeing Bahlool in combat, there was no escape possible. Bahlool then requested, and received, as his last wish a plentiful meal.

On the battlefield, a knight came out from the other side wielding his long terrible sword and asking for a combatant. The king then nodded to Bahlool to go out to meet him. Bahlool pleaded in vain. The fierce knight charged with his weapon raised to his shoulder, but Bahlool showed no sign of accepting the challenge, nor did he retreat from the face of this threatening opponent. Instead he signaled to his rival that he only wished to talk to him.

The knight ignored Bahlool's gesture and prepared to thrust forward. But as he saw no sign that Bahlool was taking a defensive posture or for that matter retreating, he was greatly amazed and thought of asking Bahlool what he wanted to talk to him about, anyway.

'I just want to ask you whether by any chance we happen to have met before, Sir?' Bahlool asked this dreadful warrior.

'No, I don't think so. Why do you ask anyway, fool?' said the dire knight.

'Or have you then ever heard of my name before, Sir?'

'No, why should I hear of some nobody's name like yours?'

'Or have you ever been looking for me in pursuit of some blood-feud, Sir?'

'All my family are safe and sound and well protected. Why do you ask all these silly questions, soldier?'

'Or do I happen to owe you something which I have failed to repay to you yet, Sir?'

'Yes! You owe me an explanation for all this stupid talk while we are in combat, horseman!'

'Yes, indeed. I just had some provisions prepared for me to eat before I depart from this world today, which I would like to share with you,' said Bahlool to his menacing foe. 'Just before you set out to slay someone entirely unknown to you and absolutely innocent of any wrong ever done to you, Sir.'

Then Bahlool drew closer to the knight until the necks of their two horses crossed. He took out the lunch from a wrapper at his side and placed it between them. And so the two enemies proceeded to enjoy their delicious meal between the two lines. The scene evoked amazement and laughter on both sides; and so being set in such a peaceful mood, the rival armies took a turn for peace on that day, as Bahlool did not wish to go to war after all.

In peace time they bury us old, in war we bury them young.

WATER

The best of drinks.

Water, greenery and a pretty face will soothe the gloomy heart.

Running water is medicine.

Out of water We have created all things alive.
– THE QUR'AN

W

WEAKNESS

Big fish eat up small fish, and the weak are doomed to perish.

Don't belittle the weakling, for a snake is doomed by the scorpion's sting.

Be not a mount for your friend, lest you both fall down.

Beware of the weapon of the weak!
[That is, their prayers to Heaven against those who wrong them.]

Weakness is not a sound excuse.
– Lilminber

WEALTH

Money is the dust of the mansion of the earth.

That Being, who increased not thy wealth,
Better than thou knew what is for thy health.
– SHEIKH SADI, thirteenth century Persian Sufi poet

Wake up early if you desire this world, and wake up early if you desire the other.
– HADITH

Wealth and children are the ornament of this world.
– THE QUR'AN

WEAPON

A weapon in a coward's hand makes a wound.

The best weapon is the one that protects you.
[...not necessarily the one that destroys your enemy.]

A loaded gun terrifies one, an unloaded one terrifies two.

WEATHER

God sends cold to every person according to their garments.
– KURDISH

If a rainbow appears in the evening, find yourself a warm corner; if in the morning, go and play in the open air; but if it spreads east and west, go and sleep at the side of the road.
– LEVANTINE

When it snows, it gets warm.
– LEVANTINE

The one bitten by cold sniffs out firewood.

She is as cold as a locust in the dew.

WEDDING

A couple weds – a whole company feasts.

Gaiety is a warm handshake.

Ahlan we-sahlan!
['You have come to your kinsfolk and have arrived in a spacious place!' The traditional Arabic greeting of welcome.]

You are welcome as many times as the steps that took you from there up to here.
– IRAQI
['Welcome' of the Iraqi countryside.]

You are invited by the acquaintances, welcomed by the friends and looked for by the beloved ones.

WIFE

Girls are glad when they look at an unhappy wife.
[Because they have no husbands yet to torment them.]

Choose your horse with your eyes, and your wife with your ears.
[Listen to what others say of her.]

A hammer's blows rather than a wife's nagging in bed.

The blind man must eat what his mad wife cooks for him.

A man's heart is like a cabbage: it is given away leaf by leaf, but the core is left for the wife.

The wedding night is honey, but the hive won't last too long.

There is a loaf for every wedding.
['Loaf' here implies chances in life for the newly married.]

From the first night he was a 'demon': he blew out the candle and lost the lighter.
– In ancient Aleppo

He married on credit, and sold his children to repay it.

The poor ones married, but the town rested in tranquillity.
[For they could not afford a clamorous party.]

Her wedding dress was sewn with his ax.
[He toiled to gather the prerequisites of married life.]

WELCOME

A kind welcome is better than a tasty dinner.

W

He who cannot oppose his mother-in-law takes revenge on his wife.

Husband of the two (co-wives) is like a neck between two sticks.

His ears are as prying as a co-wife's.

My lover carried a candle, and he ran away when my husband turned up with a torch.

WILLY-NILLY

Let me go lest I cry, hold me tight lest I fall!

When asked to fly, the ostrich said it was a camel; when asked to kneel (to be loaded), the ostrich said it was a bird.

'If I have to cook it for you, you won't find it tasty,' said the unwilling cook.

Indecision slices things in bits and pieces; decision cuts them clear.
– Lilminber

A camel's load
A camel was asked how much it would like to carry. 'Two ounces of pepper, well ground and well sifted,' it said. 'And how much by way of force?' it was then asked. 'Come and load up, let others mount and mount yourself,' replied the camel.
[A camel can carry about 660 pounds/300 kilos for a long distance, feeding mainly on wild desert herbs and plants on the way. The camel is known as the 'the ship of the desert' for the great ease and speed with which it traverses the wavy expanses of the Arabian Peninsula. It is also described as mule and horse in one and is renowned for its ability to go without water for long periods of time.]

WINE

A drunk won't count the glasses.

A little of it gladdens the heart, a little more saddens the face.

Your wisdom is already threadbare,
For you are still the son of an ape;
Wear it not yet thinner at the door of
                                    debauchery,
The devil is in every berry of the grape.
– Lilminber

But still the Vine her ancient Ruby yields,
And still a Garden by the Water blows;
Then he drowns my honor in a
                                    shallow cup,
And sold my reputation for a song.
– OMAR KHAYYAM (1048-1131), Persian mathematician, astronomer and poet

Wine does not so much corrupt a man as greed.
– KHALIF OMAR, seventh century, the second Khalif of Islam

W

In both there is great harm, and (some) benefit for men, but their harm is greater.
– THE QUR'AN
[Of gambling and wine.]

WISDOM

Wisdom surpasses power.

Head of wisdom is fear of God.

Wisdom is the tree of life.

The wise have their mouths in their hearts; fools have their hearts in their mouths.

Be wise with the ignorant and prudent with fools.

Little wisdom tires the feet.

'Our beards have turned gray, yet our wisdom is on the way,' confessed a wise man.

A fool rides a long way to and fro; a wise person steps towards a determined goal.

A wise person's guess is more certain than a fool's truth.

A wise person is like a rock: slow to warm and to cool.

A wise person's error is thousand-fold greater.

Wisdom is covered by a straw.
[It is easily visible to the seeker.]

He who learns the rules of wisdom and does not apply them in his life is like the one who labors in his field but does not sow.
– SHEIKH SADI, thirteenth century Persian Sufi poet

A person does not look for wisdom unless they are wise.

Lacking wisdom in one's own life, one may find oneself searching for it in others' thoughts and deeds.
– Lilminber

He who searches for wisdom is wise; he who thinks he has found it is a fool.
– IBN AL-ARABI, an ancient Sufi

In every head there is wisdom.

A wise person in their native town is like gold inside its mine.

Give wisdom to the fool, and you would do it injustice.

A big river flows quietly and a wise person speaks softly.
– UZBEK

W

'Who is the wise man?' someone asked Imam Ali.
'He is the one who puts things in their places,' he said.
'And who is the fool, O prince of the faithful?' he was asked again.
'I said it already,' he responded.
[Imam Ali, seventh century, was the fourth Khalif of Islam.]

The wise are the mounts of fools.
– PERSIAN

Wisdom has five phases: self-restraint, self-reliance, pursuit of knowledge, learning from the experience of others and putting to practice what is good for the community. No one on their own can attain perfect wisdom, but blessed are those who ever search for it.
– Ancient savant

The sage, whom ease and pleasure lead aside,
Is himself lost; to whom can he be guide?
– SHEIKH SADI, thirteenth century Persian Sufi poet.

Although fools in savage words themselves
express,
The wise will soothe them by their
gentleness.
– SHEIKH SADI

A wise man was asked: 'From whom should one receive wisdom?'
'From the blind,' he said,
'because they never take a step before feeling their way with a stick.'

Know all that you say but don't say all that you know.

Take wisdom (even) from the side of the road.
– HADITH

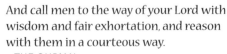

And call men to the way of your Lord with wisdom and fair exhortation, and reason with them in a courteous way.
– THE QUR'AN

WISHFUL THINKING

We sowed 'if' and reaped 'naught'.

The well is deep, but the rope is short.

The cat dreamt of catching some mice.

He licks the sky with his tongue, don't you know?

To those athirst the whole world seems
A spring of water – in their dreams.
– SHEIKH SADI, thirteenth century Persian Sufi poet

W

WITNESS

At times you look for witnesses, at times witnesses look for you.

An eye that has not seen (yet bears witness) is to be plucked twice.

She witnessed it from the knock on the door to the bidding of farewell.

The one without a witness is a liar.

'Stool witnesses'
– IRAQI
[They sit in front of public departments like courts and welfare offices in Iraq, where they are willing to sell instantly made-up testimony, usually in routine cases, like marriage documents, sales contracts and the like.]

Acquaintance with the judge is better than two witnesses.

The Day when their limbs will bear witness against them.
– THE QUR'AN
[Of sinners on Doomsday.]

WOE

God's mill grinds slow, but it grinds woe.

Woe betide the oppressors from the torments of the Day of Judgment.
– THE QUR'AN

WOMEN

A woman's advice is good for a woman.

Consult with women and do whatever you please.

Men don't like to admit women's wisdom, but they ever go back to them for counsel.

Take a woman's first advice and discard her last.

She said to the genie: 'Come... or else!'

If you play with a woman, you are already a loser.

The woman who smiles at you seeks to deceive you; the one who faces you with tears has done so already.
– EGYPTIAN

If man is a river, woman is the bridge.
– KURDISH

He who spends of his fortune to educate two daughters or sisters, Paradise will be due to him by the grace of God.
– HADITH

If a beautiful woman is a gem, a good woman is a treasure.
– PERSIAN

W

Women have shorter limbs but longer tongues.

Women are like bees: either they sting you or they give you honey.
– TURKISH

Women have love and mercy.

If she is in the mood, she would show it (even) through a brick wall.

It is better for a woman to live as a thorn than to fall as a rose.

A woman loves her man with her heart, a man loves his woman with his needs.

A woman in love is an angel living on earth.

He who hates women, hates his mother.

It is better for a woman to live with a man who loves her than with a man whom she loves.
– PERSIAN

A woman can hide her love for forty years, but not her hatred for one hour.

The wise woman has much to say, but she keeps her silence.

You may choose to be an enemy of an upright woman, but be careful when befriending a faithless one.

All married women boasted: 'I married at fourteen!'
[That is, they had admirers right from their early teens.]

Women laugh when they can and weep when they want to.

The home was not built on the ground but on the woman.

'If I'd relied on you, we wouldn't have had children, O man!'

Men without mind make women without shame.

She whose husband is by her side can turn the world with a finger.

Women are the counterparts of men; they are attire for you and you are attire for them.
– THE QUR'AN

What no longer fits a woman will fit her daughter.

One can't fill one's belly with beauty.

W

WORDS

An honest word can do for a thousand speeches.

A word from the mouth is a stone (falling) from a cliff or a flower from the garden.
– PERSIAN

A word makes you look like a fool, and a word makes you look wise.

One ties up a donkey by its feet, and a person by their tongue.

A word can reach further than a campaign.

With a true word you can face the world.

One word should do for two.

A gentle word is light on the tongue and weighty in the scale.

Some words are like an old wall – colorfully decorated, but meant to be looked at rather than be leant upon.
– Lilminber

His words were like empty nutshells.
[They made a cracking sound and were hollow.]

He who breaks a word breaks a camel.

An abdomen is large enough for a jar of hard nuts, but not for one hard word.

Whoever doesn't weigh his words will receive an answer that will vex him.
– SHEIKH SADI, thirteenth century Persian Sufi poet

Had but my deeds been like my words,
                                    ah! then,
I had been numbered, too, with holy men.
– SHEIKH SADI

WORK

Work covers the entire world.

Work in the sun – eat in the shade.

Work takes an hour, (but without it) worries take a year.

Night work ridicules the day.

Today's work is tomorrow's bread.

Hands perish; their work doesn't.

Work makes shorter days but longer life.
– TURKISH

Dig a well and fill a well, but don't let a worker stay idle.
[A bit like the 'broken glass' theory of capitalism: Break glass so that work is created for the unemployed.]

Rest after work, and work after rest.

W

It is related that the Prophet once met with a hermit who worshiped God in solitude, and asked him who provided for his living. 'My brother,' said the hermit. 'It is then your brother who is the worshiper,' said the Prophet.

Too much work earns a hernia.

The donkey died and left its packsaddle behind.
[The hardworking but greedy person left their wealth behind.]

It is the needle that spent the weaver.

Those who work the hardest will gain the least.

The baker stands with fire in front of him and shouts from behind.
– MOROCCAN

WORLD

The world is a mirror: it looks at you the same way you look at it.

The world is being ruined everyday, but builders are always at work rebuilding it.

The world can be shaken but not felled.

The world is but an aba-robe: one day it is under you, another day it is over you, but it stays always with you.
[The aba is a traditional flowing overcoat, which has many functions.]

The world is our single mother, and we are all her screaming bastards.
– LEVANTINE

A boy's work might be good, but no one is happy with it.

One foot on the barren soil, the other on the fertile soil.
[Some work with only half their ability.]

Marry a worker, rather than an inheritor.

We wander seeking pasture, and that is our work.
– BEDOUIN

If your scythe is broken, make a sickle out of it.
– MOROCCAN

Work straightens out faults and consolidates knowledge.
– Lilminber

Work is prayer.
– HADITH

Pay a toiler his wage before his sweat is dry.
– HADITH

W

Purchase the next World with this one, and thus shalt thou win both.
– HADITH

WORRY

Worries were asked how they entered. 'Through the open door,' they answered.

Had mountains men's worries, they would have collapsed.

He dealt with worries by pouring blood on them.
[Of keeping worries at bay with hard work.]

I said to worries, 'Go away!' 'We feel better on your shoulder,' they said to me.

The dead were once dug up, and it was found out that two-thirds of the world died from (groundless) worries.

Worries of the world are many, yet they are divided and shared.
[...not quite equally, though.]

Big heads, big headaches.

Cares are a burden on the road; lighten them by carrying less of them.

The world is like a dancing girl: it dances a little bit for everyone in turn.

The world shows you the horse and gives you the donkey.

If in this world you are a drummer, you will be a flautist in the hereafter.

The world will end up in an uproar, anyway.

Early to bed if you want to win this world, and early to bed if you want to win the next one.
– HADITH

Seek I for goods which not to me belong;
Then if men call me worldly they're not wrong.
– SHEIKH SADI, thirteenth century Persian Sufi poet

Lo! Lightning does grin in choler,
And the clouds do cry in the flare;
I shall leave thee, ye cheerless world,
For a saint or a devil, I won't care.
– ABUL ALAA AL-MA'RRI, eleventh century poet

Take care not to let cares take you.

Joy comes by the beloved, cares come by the beloved.

He who possesses a mill and an orchard and has children and a wife will never go through a quiet night throughout his life.

Fear is true, worries are false.

He who has no heart will die fat.
[He who has no worried heart will die happy.]

She who weeps for the whole world will end up blind.
[OR: O, ye who bear others' cares! To whom have you left your own, anyway?]

As he had no worries, Bahlool cut off his nose and looked for medicine with which to heal it.

WRITING

Write down before you forget.

What a great thing, the pen: it weaves the warp and weft of the kingdom so fine.
– KHALIF AL-MA'MOON of Baghdad, tenth century

Pens are the mouths of thoughts.

What a wonder is the pen: it drinks darkness and utters light.

Writers' pens are sharper than warriors' swords.

Write down the best of what you hear, and learn by heart the best of what you write, and speak the best of what you learn by heart.
– IBN UL-MUQAFFA tenth century

It is the audience who create the speaker, and the readers who write the books.
– Lilminber

Writing down fine thoughts is like weaving a beautiful carpet.
– SHEIKH SADI, thirteenth century Persian Sufi poet

WRONG

You who did wrong yesterday, do right today!

There is no one who is always wrong: even a broken clock is right twice a day.
– TURKISH

To do the right thing in the wrong way is an apprentice's act; to do wrong in the right way is the Devil's business, but to do the right thing in the right way befits the wise.
– PERSIAN

Be wrong with everybody rather than be lonely in the right.
[OR: If you want to have peace of mind, always say: Never mind!]

You are the best community that has been raised for humankind, for you proclaim right conduct and forbid the wrong.
– THE QUR'AN

Y & Z

A bad year has twenty-four months.

YEAR

A good Spring ushers in a good year.

Shorten your days and your years will be longer.
[Do not allow yourself to be consumed with overwork.]

YES & NO

Yes-men cry with every crow, bark with every dog, bray with every ass – anything but speak their minds.

No after Yes is but a decline,
Yes after No is just fine.

Y & Z

YOUTH

Burn your way through with youth's fire,
Before the warm veins chill in vain;
Torch of wisdom, lit up by young souls
Lightens the burden and lights up the lane.
– ABUL ALAA AL-MA'RRI, eleventh century poet

Alas, the page of youth is folded up,
That fresh spring of life drained away;
The bird of pleasure, whose name is Youth,
Rose a moment, flapped a wing and
                                went its way.
– FIRDOUSI, twelfth century Persian author of
the epic *Shahnama*

Neither a sultan nor a bey can stand in youth's
way.
– TURKISH
['Bey' was a title of authority during the Ottoman era.]

Youth are welcome to talk and the old to
listen and guide.

The sage whose bright mind mirrors truth,
May sometimes wander wide of it:
While, by mistake, the simple youth,
Will, with his shaft, target it.
– SHEIKH SADI, thirteenth century Persian Sufi
poet

ZEAL

A person without zeal is a person without
religion.
– LEVANTINE

Zeal is the warmth of life. We need to extract
light from it to lighten our path.
– Lilminber

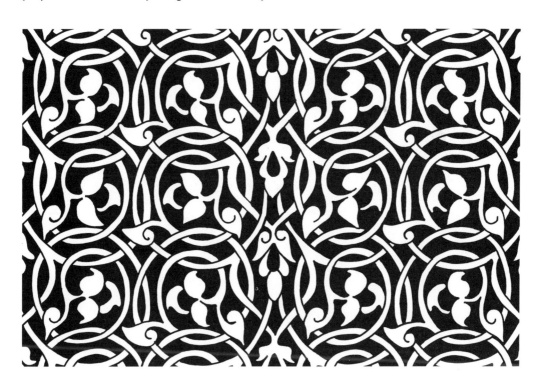

ABOUT THE AUTHOR

HUSSAIN MOHAMMED AL-AMILY was born in 1927 in Najaf, Iraq to a Lebanese clergy father and an Iraqi mother. He spent his formative years in both countries. He is widely traveled in the Arabic world and has lived in France, Germany and lastly Britain, where he currently resides. In his early years he was a wandering preacher among the peoples of Iraq for whom he has great affection, but later developed a trade business. A founder member of the Iraqi Translators' Society, Baghdad, he has authored several works and contributed many articles for Western and other magazines on Arabic culture and general affairs. He is also a life member of the Universal Esperanto Association promoting the international language, Esperanto, and has consultative relations with UNESCO.